USING RESEARCH IN ORGANIZATIONS

Volume 101, Sage Library of Social Research

Research Techniques

(S) SAGE LIBRARY OF SOCIAL RESEARCH

USING RESEARCH IN ORGANIZATIONS

A Guide to Successful Application

Jack Rothman

Foreword by **Ronald G. Havelock**

*Published in cooperation with the National Institute of
Social Work, London, and the Center for Research on Utilization
of Scientific Knowledge, Institute of Social Research, University of
Michigan.*

Volume 101
SAGE LIBRARY OF
SOCIAL RESEARCH

 SAGE Publications   Beverly Hills   London

For information address:

SAGE Publications, Inc.
275 South Beverly Drive
Beverly Hills, California 90212

SAGE Publications Ltd
28 Banner Street
London EC1Y 8QE, England

Printed in the United States of America

Library of Congress Cataloging in Publication Data

Rothman, Jack.
    Using research in organizations.

    (Sage library of social research ; v. 101)
    Bibliography: p.
    Includes index.
    1. Evaluation research (Social action programs)
2. Evaluation research (Social action programs)—
Great Britain. I. Title.
H62.R677   658.4'03'072   79-27947
ISBN 0-8039-1442-3
ISBN 0-8039-1443-1 pbk.

FIRST PRINTING

CONTENTS

ACKNOWLEDGMENTS

I am writing these acknowledgments on the eve of Thanksgiving; a most appropriate happenstance. For only the author fully knows the extent to which he is indebted to others in the creation and production of a book such as this. Especially in an old-fashioned research endeavor, where a single investigator works without institutional funding, the freely given generosity and support of others is critical at many points along the way.

The study on which the book is based was conducted during a sabbatical leave which I spent in London. The Fulbright-Hayes United Kingdom Sponsoring Commission provided vital assistance in meeting some of the living expenses of my family. Mr J. O. E. Herrington, Secretary of the Commission, was an unusually gracious host, serving as welcoming committee, advisor, and paternal overseer.

I was especially fortunate to be offered an affiliation, including office accommodation, at the National Institute for Social Work in London. David Jones, Principal of the Institute, was ever available as a consultant on the study. His, incredible storehouse of information and contacts was an invaluable aid. He counseled on the selection of study sites, suggested names of numerous individuals to serve in resource capacities, and provided entrée whenever this was needed or desirable. Priscilla Foley of the Institute staff was the perfect secretary: My letters went out accurately and on time; my questionnaires were mimeographed with precision; directions for travel by bus, tube, train, and on foot to the various places I was to visit within London and in the surrounding area were always ready for me and clearly spelled out. Whenever I got lost it was entirely my own fault. The other members of the Institute faculty and staff were a congenial and stimulating influence regarding professional and general matters. Without notable success, I have attempted to transpose some of the lovely atmosphere of the commons room at the Institute to the faculty lounge of my school back here at the university.

The administrators and senior researchers who were interviewed in field agencies provided the raw material on which this analysis was built. These were busy professionals experiencing varying levels of overload. Still, they lent themselves to the study, sharing their experiences and reflections in interview sessions ordinarily occupying two hours of time or more. The importance of their cooperation to the completion of the undertaking cannot be overstated.

Some of the other individuals in Britain who were kind enough to react to the study and discuss related aspects of the social services or research utilization in Britain include the following: Professor Adrian L. Webb of the University of Loughborough, Professor Brian Abel-Smith of the London School of Economics, Mr William Utting of the Department of Health and Social Security, Professor Robert Pinker of the University of London, Dr Cyril S. Smith of the Social Science Research Council, Mr A. R. Isserlis of the Centre for Studies in Social Policy, Professor Albert Cherns of the University of Loughborough, and Mr David Plank of the Greater London Council. Their assistance and that of others speeded up considerably the period of orientation of a stranger on the scene and allowed me to proceed with my work in an all the more informed way.

The analysis and write-up of the study was carried forward in my home institution, the University of Michigan. Here the contribution of Vivian Roeder, filling multiple roles of secretary, research assistant, and general aide, demands to be noted. Vivian left her imprint in varied ways, demonstrating competence, loyalty, and friendship of a special kind. The Center for Research on the Utilization of Scientific Knowledge (CRUSK) of the Institute for Social Research at the University of Michigan, through a Faculty Associate appointment, freed a block of uninterrupted time which I devoted to completing the analysis and drafting the manuscript. Dr Donald Pelz, Director of CRUSK at that time, closely reviewed the first draft and made innumerable critical comments and suggestions that, I believe, have led to a significantly improved presentation. Another CRUSK staff member, Nathan Caplan, shared with me a questionnaire he had used in studying research utilization among federal policy makers, and suggested changes based on experiences in using it. This questionnaire, as adapted, became the main data-gathering instrumentality of the study. Mimi Horne of CRUSK typed an interim version of the manuscript while having to contend with elliptical notes and a new word processing machine. My editorial consultant and assistant in a number of publishing ventures, Gershom Clark Morningstar, prepared the final version of this manuscript with his usual professional aplomb and proficiency.

My family should also receive their due for kindly tolerating and accepting an often intense and preoccupied husband and father through this period and many another.

These individuals parade behind me like the figures from the past who trail Quentin across the stage in Arthur Miller's "After the Fall." To the naked eye, only the main character is visible; through the vision of the playwright we are able to observe the significant others who have had a role in the formation of Quentin's present self. My performance likewise required supporting players. Perhaps on this evening I will be forgiven if I stretch a point and liken the scene to a

Thanksgiving Day parade. For to this lineup of benefactors I owe a heavy debt of thanks.

Ann Arbor, Michigan   *Jack Rothman*
November 1979

FOREWORD

Few managers in today's world would question the importance of good information as the basis of good decision-making. Yet there is considerably less consensus on what constitutes "good" information, where it comes from, and how it can be used. This book is designed to help. The premise is that evaluation research *can be* useful to management *if* attention is paid to the process of research utilization by both the manager and the researcher. Rothman goes on from here to tell us in fairly specific terms what this process is and how we can attend to it to make the research better and to make its use better.

Rothman believes, as I do, that the process of research utilization has been a sorely neglected topic in the social sciences. The old-fashioned concept of knowledge transfer went something like this: "Build a better mousetrap and the world will beat a path to your door." In other words, the dissemination and use of research was supposed to depend primarily on the goodness or intrinsic worth of the research itself. Only gradually over the last generation have we begun to realize that such an attitude almost guarantees the nonutilization of most research. Our growing awareness of what it takes to get the most out of the research enterprise has come in part from years of frustration, but it has also come from the efforts of a few social scientists to turn their methods and skills on the problem itself, the problem of the dissemination and utilization of research. This volume admirably summarizes and integrates a number of these studies, but more importantly, it attempts to shape their conclusions to a useful purpose. For this is essentially written as a handbook and guide for the administrator and the researcher. It allows them to examine their present practice and their present orientation to each other in a systematic way that should show where the gaps are and where the strengths are that they can build on.

The basic heuristic model that Rothman follows is the "two-world" model, the notion that the world of research and the world of administrative practice have essential differences in language, values, methods, and points of view. Of course, this is a simplification. We all know that there are many "worlds" in this sense, mostly overlapping and not well defined, but the imposition of the two-world model allows us to sharpen a number of issues which are important. Most importantly, this approach tends to focus our attention on the issue of *communication* between persons and between systems. Research is used when there is effective communication between the research generator and the research user. Effective communication, however, is not a one-way process; rather, it is a dialogue which takes place over time, which allows a full sharing of concerns on both sides, and which allows for the reshaping of the message to suit the needs, concerns, and circumstances of the receiver.

The linkage model of research utilization reflected in this book suggests that there is a number of types of communication which should take place between the researcher and the user. The most obvious of these is the *transfer* of technical knowledge, skill, and expertise from the researcher to the user. In part this is a matter of putting together a good, readable, and well-packaged product, a matter which Rothman covers nicely in Chapter 5. But the transfer process involves much more than this: It involves various kinds of transformations, summarizations, and interpretations for different members of the using organization; many of these issues are discussed in Chapter 3. Yet effective transfer is only part of the story; effective utilization usually requires that the user participate in the knowledge-building process at various stages. First of all, the user and the *user's concerns* should have some influence in defining the problem and setting the objectives for research; thus, users' needs must be articulated and communicated. At later stages when the knowledge products are being shaped and tested for the first time, there must be a considerable amount of additional input from the user in the form of reactions and comments on perceived relevance, utility, and feasibility. The process factors discussed in Chapter 3 speak to these points.

Linkage is not merely a matter of sending and receiving, however. It requires or assumes the *internalization* of messages on both sides, and this means that each must devote considerable *effort* to the activity of communicating, especially at the early stages of a relationship. In developing such a relationship there will inevitably be resistance and conflict, some of which can be resolved but some of which derives from the nature of each role. Empathy means understanding and having a feeling and appreciation for the other; it does not mean surrendering one's identity or submerging one's self-interest and legitimate role concerns to the other. Empathy and trust between the researcher and the manager is something that must build up over many encounters, formal and informal.

Creating situations which allow for these many encounters is not always easy. In the cases for which Rothman provides the most data, there are certain givens which do make this more likely. Structurally, the research units are generally subparts of a larger organization and most likely housed within the same buildings within reasonable *proximity* of the managers. In situations where this is not the case, even greater effort needs to be invested in creating mechanisms and social settings which bring the two together on a routine basis.

The focus of this book is on one key interface: between applied evaluation research and management within a bureaucracy. This fact should not mislead the reader into thinking that either the problems or the solutions proposed by Rothman are unique to this interface. On the contrary, the same principles apply generally to the problem of research utilization across situations, including those in which researcher and manager belong to different organizations and have different institutional loyalties. They apply when the research to be utilized is of a "hard" and technological character as well as when it is derived from the social sciences. They also apply when the "user" is someone other than the manager, e.g., a professional practitioner, a legislator, a policy maker, or a researcher in another field. The basic need is to provide the decision maker or the practitioner with all the expert knowledge that each can effectively use regarding a particular problem, setting, or situation, regardless of its source. This book represents a useful step in that direction.

It is important for us to recognize that there is a gap between the world of research and the world of routine organizational practice, regardless of the field. Once we recognize the gap there are three things which can be done about it. The first is to *legitimize* whatever efforts are undertaken by anyone to close the gap. The second is to provide *resources* in people, time, and funds to support a variety of linkage efforts. The third is to plan and structure linkage-building activities in a thoughtful and systematic way. Rothman's book points out the importance of these three aspects and provides us with very good starting guidelines on the third point. We can only hope that a rising tide of awareness and concern for better use of research will provide the legitimation and resources that a book in itself cannot provide.

— *Ronald G. Havelock*
Director
Knowledge Transfer Institute
The American University
Washington, D.C.

Chapter 1

INTRODUCTION

Growth in scope and influence of the social sciences is an evident contemporary trend. Social research studies of all kinds have proliferated, and social scientists in increased numbers inhabit not only universities but governmental bodies, private agencies, and corporate establishments. A concurrent development has been expansion of social programs, given impetus by both the growing complexity of social problems and the predilection of modern governments to attack these problems through use of public authority in a planned, organized way.

While there is general agreement about advances in the quantity and quality of social science research, much disquiet exists about whether this accumulating knowledge is having a reasonable impact on the design and implementation of social programs. A special study commission of a U.S. scientific bureau examined this issue nationally. The team concluded that:

At present, the social sciences...are a relatively unused national resource. Much of America's effort to achieve its aims makes little attempt to use this fundamental resource. The Commission asserts its doubt that the country can successfully solve its diverse social problems unless it draws upon the increasing capabilities of the social science community [National Science Foundation, 1969: 4].

The matter is illuminated in discussions by two British social scientists. Sharpe (1975), a professor of political science at Oxford, is dubious concerning prospects of research finding its way into the operational field of policy making. He is of the opinion that there has been "over-optimism" on this score, and he alludes to a number of obstacles that enthusiasts have not sufficiently taken into account: Policy makers sometimes do not wish to be well informed because their decision-making may become more complicated; much research is too abstract to assist policy makers in dealing with specific practical problems; policy makers find it difficult to accept research that refutes common opinion; the time scale for research is too extensive to meet the short-term needs of applied people.

A more hopeful point of view is expressed by Donnison (1972), a respected academic from the London School of Economics, who has also served at high governmental levels as a policy maker and administrator in the British social services. According to Donnison, research perspectives can and do infuse the policy-making process. This comes about indirectly and informally, however, through a network of interlocking associations among intellectuals, journalists, and governmental officials. It is a complex, convoluted process that works delicately and unpredictably. Even Donnison's positive stance leaves one with a sense of uncertainty. Neither Sharpe nor Donnison envision research ordinarily having an organic relationship and short-term impact on social plans and programs.

In part this assessment is filtered through an implicit definition of research reflected by both observers. A close reading shows that they are speaking primarily of academic or basic research, conducted by faculty in university settings and dealing with broad theoretical issues. Donnison acknowledges, however, that there is a range of different types of research: mission-oriented research, nonmission or basic research, development and application. Unfortunately, the term research has become enveloped in conceptual confusion, to the extent that one skeptic has commented, "a schoolboy, looking up a word in a dictionary is now said to be doing research." This has impeded discerning analysis.

It is useful to make distinctions between different modalities of research and their differential interface with the problems of application. Cherns (1970) has suggested four different forms of research:

Pure basic research — theoretical and knowledge producing in nature.

Basic objective research — basic research arising out of some field of application of the discipline, but not aimed at prescribing a solution to a problem.

Operations research — research aimed at solving ongoing problems within organizational settings.

Action research — research that incorporates a strategy for the introduction of planned change.

Other schemes have been advanced, none of which is universally accepted among students of the subject. Essentially, the Cherns formulation divides into two forms of basic research and two forms of applied research, with distinctions within each of the categories somewhat unclear and overlapping. The rough, twofold, basic/applied conception is widely accepted and serviceable for our purposes.

Essentially, it is important to recognize that the model of pure research that has dominated academic and scholarly writing in the social sciences represents only one of several research orientations and technologies. It is with this mode of research that application is most problematic. Counterposed to pure or basic research is program evaluation and operations research — research that has its focus within a given organizational setting and is geared to concrete problem-solving goals. Its purpose is to enable a given organization to function in a more effective way in meeting its intended objectives, rather than to accumulate generalized knowledge about the social world.

This organizationally based, pragmatic approach to research will be the focus of this book. Evaluation research, as envisioned here, is broad in scope. It involves the conducting of any kind of research within an organization to acquire intelligence that can be fed back in order to enable the organization to improve its functioning. It overlaps with operations research in that it entails such organizational inquiries as needs assessments, descriptive information about services to clients, the tracking of clients, task analyses of professional activities, cost/benefit analysis, and so on. The term will include whatever research efforts contribute to the effectiveness of a particular organization's performance in serving clients and meeting community needs. Appendix B documents provide such a view.

Smith (1972) presents theoretical argumentation to the effect that evaluation research units within human service organizations are capable of having a more direct and practical effect on program outputs than is university-based research. Elsewhere, in their study of research by federal policy makers in the United States, Caplan et al. (1975) report that overwhelmingly, government officials relied on focused research conducted within the agency ("in-house") and made good use of such information. This more-applied perspective on research appears to brighten the pessimistic outlook of the earlier commentators.

Nevertheless, even here one must take pause. The professional journals and agency coffee rooms are replete with laments concerning the dead-end trajectory of many in-house research studies. Churchman (1964:33), writing from the point of view of industrial operations research, states:

Some of my graduate students undertook to write to the authors of cases reported in *Operations Research* over the first six years of its publication to determine to what extent the recommendations of the studies had been carried out by management. In no case was there sufficient evidence that the recommendations had been accepted.

Evaluation research fares no better. Numerous authors have cataloged myriad reasons for the failure of organizations to use evaluation (Agarwala-Rogers, 1977; Goldstein et al., 1978; Guba, 1975; Knezo, 1974; Wilson, 1978). Ironically, Scanlon and Waller (1978) provide evidence showing that utilization, when it occurs, can materially *improve* social programs, and Patton (1978:291), in assessing the benefits of evaluation research, makes a dramatic plea for its use:

> Utilization focused evaluation may, indeed, be a long shot, but the potential payoff is worth the risk. At stake is improving the effectiveness of human service programs that express and embody the highest ideals of mankind.

An evaluation research formulation is clearly not a panacea for integrating information-gathering and operational practices. There is reason to believe that in-house evaluation increases the potential for utilization but that it falls short of bringing about maximal use levels. In the discussions that follow, our endeavour will be to explore how these use levels might be raised. First, however, the relationship between research knowledge and its application will be conceptualized, drawing in particular on the notion of linkage. Greater conceptual clarity is needed in this realm, which has to a large degree been dominated by intuition.

LINKAGE BETWEEN RESEARCH AND APPLICATION

Taking the research function as our point of departure, research utilization may be conceived of as involving movement across the space between producers of knowledge (researchers) and users of knowledge (appliers). Ideally, this should be a smooth process with few impediments. The researcher should be eager to create and pass on validated knowledge that will be practical and appreciated.

In reality, compatibility of purposes and outlook between the two sets of actors, necessary for expeditious conveyance of research, can hardly be said to exist. Rather than allied colleagues, Caplan's data (1977) suggest the existence of "two communities" composed of separate and somewhat alien camps. Rosenblatt (1968) found that social work practitioners have a low level of knowledge about research and consider it one of the last places to turn to for sources of guidance to practice. In studying teachers and educational researchers, Joly (1967) was led to characterize them as "two solitudes." On the basis of an extensive review of pertinent literature, the following appear to be important areas of dissonance between knowledge producers and knowledge appliers: conflicting values, orientations toward clients, languages, methodological assumptions, role perceptions, focal objectives and concerns, definitions of professional ethics, and identifications (see Rothman, 1974).

It has become evident that the space between researcher and applier represents a gap comprised of intellectual, social, emotional, and (usually) physical distance, with numerous barriers to knowledge transfer and few facilitating linkages. The notion of linkage will be reviewed in order to illustrate dimensions of the linkage formulation.

Linkage can be analyzed in terms of the source of initiation of communication. The researcher might transmit findings to the user. The user might advance upon the researcher and seize his or her product. They might converge in middle ground. Alternatively, a third party might move between the two. Some of these patterns have been discussed by Lippitt and Havelock (1968). In order to foster such initiation, it has been advocated, on the one hand, that users become better consumers of research (Rogers, 1967), or, on the other, that researchers become more assertive and sensitive in disseminating their findings (Glaser 1973). A reformulation of the process could involve the researcher and applier as joint participants at the outset of a research undertaking. Initiation would then be from a collaborative researcher/applier team to other appliers. If one's analysis does not start with a research focus, as in this work, it is obvious that the impetus for research can originate from many sources — policy makers, managers, community groups, practitioners, clients, political influentials, and others.

A number of students of the subject have concluded that communication, itself, cannot be relied upon to achieve utilization (Halpert, 1966; Schwartz, 1966). A variety of linking procedures and mechanisms have been suggested as necessary in order to bring about appropriate coupling. One approach entails improving attitudes among the parties and encouraging mutual association (Likert and Lippitt, 1963). A sensitivity training program involving T-group experiences has been outlined for achieving this end (Schmuck, 1968).

The use of an intermediary linking agent has been advocated by a large number of observers. Such a mediating individual has been described by use of such diverse terms as *social intermediary* (Coleman et al., 1966), *informed colleague and gatekeeper* (Roberts and Larsen, 1971), *field agent* (Sieber et al., 1974), *social engineer* (Rothman, 1980), and, simply, *middleman* (Guetzkow, 1959). Certain subroles and functions of linking agents have also been explicated. For example, Short (1973) speaks of the "integrator," the "translator," and the "knowledge linker" as specialized linking roles. Lundberg (1966) delineates different "conversion" roles, including the "technician," the "professional"(or theoretically oriented practitioner), and the "applied scientist." Necessary characteristics of the linking agent have been noted; for example, possession of training in both the method of research and the art of utilization (Glock, 1961). Indeed, it has been suggested by Carter (1968) that linking agents should be viewed as representing a new professional discipline that performs social engineering functions.

Beyond roles and personages, wider perspectives on linkage have been advanced. One envisages intermediary institutions or agencies that function as specialized linking organizations (National Science Foundation, 1969). Havelock has developed the concept of multidimensional linking systems (Havelock and Markowitz, 1973; Havelock and Lingwood, 1973). A complex research utilization linking process, employing systematic R & D procedures, has also been set forth (Rothman, 1980).

In the present study many of these modes of linkage were identified. Patterns that were discovered could be grouped expediently under four categories of linkage:

(1) structural arrangements facilitating linkage
(2) linking processes and procedures
(3) attitudes and interrelationships
(4) characteristics of research reports and products

These categories will form the basic structure of this book. We found some overlap among the categories; for example, a mechanism having structural properties may also serve as an instrumentality of process; or a particular attitudinal characteristic may be taken into account in composing a research report. For this reason, there is a certain amount of redundancy across linkage categories. We have chosen to tolerate such reiteration in the interests of giving a comprehensive and self-contained treatment of each linkage category. Before entering into the substantive discussion, we will briefly describe the method employed for obtaining the data that constitute the basis for the analysis.

STUDYING THE RESEARCH UTILIZATION PROCESS

In this book we will direct our attention, ultimately, to how linkage between research and its application can be enhanced. We will explore ways of structuring and carrying out the research function within an organization so as to maximize the probability of research findings being used by the organization in its operations. In order to arrive at an understanding of the phenomenon, a study was conducted in which the main individual responsible for research and the main individual responsible for application within the same organization were interviewed regarding their experiences in putting research to work. Of particular interest were their views about how this could best be brought about. Thus, a representative from each of the "alien camps" was asked to assess a common utilization experience in the same organization.

We did not design the study to investigate again the frequently examined question of whether research is or is not used in agency operations, or to what degree it is used. We assumed that some research is used, and a great deal is not. The questions that interested us were: "What conditions are associated with greater utilization? When research *is* used, what accounts for that happening?"

The study was conducted in twelve British Social Service Departments in and around Greater London (inner boroughs, outer boroughs, and home counties) where productive research utilization was in evidence. The departments were selected through interviews with a panel of ten knowledgeable experts familiar with the operations of these departments: recognized academics, local researchers, local department directors, national-level researchers, and national-level agency executives. The experts were asked to name departments in the region where a relatively greater degree of effective research utilization was taking place, and where there were able professionals who had given concentrated attention to this matter.

Through this design we attempted to locate more "ideal"

situations, characterized by a relatively greater degree of successful research utilization. We interviewed key informants within each of these settings, asking them to indicate those variables they viewed as conducive to positive research utilization in their organization.

British Social Service Departments are uniquely and ideally suited to the study of research utilization. They are structured in such a way that each agency is staffed with a senior research officer in addition to a chief administrator. In each of these agencies, therefore, there is a vector (of varying intensity) of research and another of administrative process.

In this study occupants of both positions (research and administrative) were interviewed in 12 social service departments (out of a possible 37 geographic units located in the study region) that had attained high rates of nomination for inclusion by the knowledgeable panel, and where access could be obtained. In all, 24 informants participated.

The sample agencies should not be viewed as representing perfect examples in an absolute sense. The interviews revealed that many of the basic problems of linkage between researchers and operational people existed in these situations, organizational structures notwithstanding. There was in these settings, however, a more enlightened view of the question and greater willingness to expend energy to find solutions.

The interviewer (the author) employed a structured questionnaire that contained mostly openended items. The procedure was flexible, permitting respondents to develop their thoughts at length and to move freely from idea to idea. Most interviews were lengthy, averaging over two hours — occasionally taking as many as four hours. Once the interview had begun, the common experience was that respondents were eager to talk, especially the research staff members. The interviewer took detailed notes during the interview, recording and expanding on these in the period immediately following. When a particularly apt statement was made, the respondent was asked to repeat it so that the exact wording could be recorded. The quotes that appear in this report approximate the comments made by the participants, either as exact statements or close paraphrases. The two forms of response are not separated in the presentation. The reader should, therefore, take them generally as *close approximations of the verbal responses.*

Respondents were asked to recall an instance in which a specific research study was used as the basis for a planning decision within the agency. They were then urged to trace the influences involved in such a successful case of utilization. They were asked on a more general level, "Do you feel there are factors that work in favor of, or against, the use of social research information in your organization? What are the factors that work for the use of such information? What are the factors that work against the use of such information?" A general question was also put to respondents concerning suggestions for improving research utilization and for improving the relationships between researchers and operational people. Because of the fluidity of the interview situations, the more general questions in some instances became the main source of data. (The questionnaire can be found in Appendix A.)

We discovered that in most instances the responses of the chief administrative officers and the researchers were not markedly different. We have, therefore, grouped their responses together, indicating general patterns of responses. Where specific differences were found, these are indicated.

The analysis of the questionnaire data involved an informal content analysis conducted by the investigator. In reviewing responses, each specific concept about research utilization mentioned by a respondent, whether a few words or a paragraph, was identified and delineated through underlining. By examining the full set of responses so designated, the fourfold analytic framework (which is reflected by the four data chapters of this book) was developed inductively. Each concept was then coded with respect to as many of the categories of the framework that applied. Subcategories were subsequently constructed on the same inductive basis.

The methodology is one of a variety of different approaches that might be employed for studying this subject. Weiss (1977) has referred to this method as "a direct survey about use of research." She lists seven other procedures that might be used as alternatives:

(1) case studies of research that has or has not been used
(2) field experiments in promoting the acceptance of research
(3) presenting actual studies to decision makers to obtain responses from them about potential usefulness
(4) presenting simulated research studies to decision makers to gauge their view of usefulness of systematically varied factors
(5) tracing a policy decision back to its research roots
(6) keeping systematic logs of requests for studies or for information
(7) participation of researchers in decision making as consultants or decision makers

Weiss indicates that none of the methods is inherently superior to any of the others. Advantages and disadvantages of each can be explicated, for each provides a different order of information; e.g., behavioral responses in an actual utilization situation, or opinional responses about usefulness of studies. The opinion approach can have wider scope while the field experiment provides depth and variety in a limited context. For the purposes of the exploratory study undertaken in this instance, the survey approach seemed appropriate. The fact that it treats opinions rather than actual behavior must be recognized in assessing our conclusions.

To sharpen the context of the study, we were examining how information moved *within* the organization from the place where it was gathered to the place where it was used, from research functionaries to operational functionaries (managers and practitioners). We were not treating the question of how research entered the organization from *outside* and from what sources. In particular, we were focusing on those variables that facilitate linkage of research information among relevant actors within the same organization. Analogues are community mental health centers having a research and evaluation unit, city planning commissions, school districts, public welfare departments, corporations, and a multiplicity of federal bureaus.

The agencies that participated in the study were engaged in a wide variety of research undertakings. Those discussed in the interviews may be generally categorized as follows:

Broad Assessment of Needs Related to Resources in a Functional Field of Service

Example: A study of the needs of the elderly within an agency's general geographic service area.

Example: A study of the needs of children under five years of age within an agency's general geographic area of service.

Specific Assessment of Needs Related to Resources in a Delimited Functional Field of Service or Geographic Area

This was the most frequent type of study and included home help supports for the elderly, group homes for the elderly, foster care services for children, hostel facilities for runaway or homeless adolescents, day care provisions for young children, and leisure and recreational activities for school-aged children.

Studies of Organizational Effectiveness in Delivering Services Generally

Example: A study of the organization of the total personal service division in order to improve its productivity and effectiveness in delivering community-based services.

Example: A study of the size, composition, and level of staffing of all area teams operating at the neighbourhood level.

Studies of Organizational Effectiveness in Delivering a Delimited Service

Example: A study of the managerial control and financial accountability in provision of aids and adaptations to physically handicapped individuals in their own homes.

Studies of Patterns of Service Delivery

Example: Equalizing the distribution of services within the agency's service area so that one region is not overserved and another underserved.

Example: Locating specific sites for day centers as services are expanded.

Examining Specific Service Questions That Arise

Example: What is the best way to establish small-group residential facilities for the elderly?

Example: How should independent living arrangements be arranged for small groups of mentally retarded clients who are released from large institutions?

Example: Are there too many children in residential care?

Appendix B2 indicates a constellation of research conducted in a single agency in a program year. In Appendix B4 there may be found a job description of the Senior Research Officer.

Our study is qualitative and exploratory in design, and is intended to have a heuristic function in generating ideas about how to improve research utilization. It was hoped that a series of fruitful hypotheses about effective linkages would be produced by going to those individuals who were rather successful in achieving linkage and obtaining from them their perspectives on the process. The actual words of the respondents will be relied upon substantially to reflect their thoughts and recommendations and to portray the research utilization phenomenon in considerable richness. There will be a stance of extensivity in attempting to encompass a broad range of independent variables that may have positive effects on utilization of research within an organization. Tendencies and useful ideas will be set forth, without an attempt to quantify or weigh. These should provide the basis for further and more refined study. Because of the qualitative character of our material and the small sample, we have drawn extensively on other studies in the literature of research utilization in order to amplify what was brought out in our own investigation. The integration of a considerable number of related studies from the existing literature has served to strengthen the findings from this particular investigation.

REFERENCES

AGARWALA-ROGERS, REHKA (1977) "Why is evaluation research not utilized?" in Marcia Guttentag (ed.) Evaluation Studies Review Annual, Vol. 2. Beverly Hills, CA: Sage.

CAPLAN, NATHAN (1977) "A minimal set of conditions necessary for the utilization of social science knowledge in policy formulation at the national level," pp. 183-197 in Carol H. Weiss (ed.) Using Social Research in Public Policy Making. Lexington, MA: D. C. Heath.

——— A. MORRISON and R. STAMBAUGH (1975) The Use of Social Science Knowledge in Policy Decisions at the National Level: A Report to Respondents. Ann Arbor: Institute for Social Research, University of Michigan.

CARTER, LAUNOR F. (1968) "Knowledge production and utilization in contemporary organizations" pp. 1-20 in T. L. Eidell and J. M. Kitchel (eds.) Knowledge Production and Utilization in Educational Administration. Eugene: Center for the Advanced Study of Educational Administration, University of Oregon.

CHERNS, ALBERT B. (1970) "Relations between research institutions and users of research." International Social Science Journal 22, 2: 226-242.

CHURCHMAN, C. WEST (1964) "Managerial acceptance of scientific recommendations." California Management Review 7, 1: 31-38.

COLEMAN, J. S., E. KATZ, and H. MENZEL (1966) Medical Innovations: A Diffusion Study. Indianapolis: Bobbs-Merrill.

DONNISON, DAVID (1972) "Research for policy." Minerva 10, 4: 519-536.

GLASER, EDWARD M. (1973) "Knowledge transfer and institutional change." Professional Psychology 4: 434-444.

GLOCK, CHARLES Y. (1961) "Applied social research: some conditions affecting its utilization," pp. 1-19 in Case Studies in Bringing Behavioral Science into Use: Studies in the Utilization of Behavioral Science, Vol. 1. Stanford, CA: Institute for Communication Research, Stanford University.

GOLDSTEIN, MICHAEL S., ALFRED C. MARCUS, and NANCY P. RAUSCH (1978) "The nonutilization of evaluation research." Pacific Sociological Review 21, 1: 21-44.

GUBA, EGON G. (1975) "Problems in utilizing the results of evaluation." Journal of Research and Development in Education 8, 3: 42-54.

——— (1968) "Development, diffusion and evaluation," pp. 37-63 in T. L. Eidell and J. M. Kitchel (eds.) Knowledge Production and Utilization in Educational Administration. Eugene: Center for the Advanced Study of Educational Administration, University of Oregon.

GUETZKOW, HAROLD (1959) "Conversion barriers in using the social sciences." Administrative Science Quarterly 4: 68-81.

HALPERT, HAROLD P. (1966) "Communication as a basic tool in promoting utilization of research findings." Community Mental Health Journal 2, 3: 231-236.

HAVELOCK, RONALD G. and E. A. MARKOWITZ (1973) Highway Safety Research Communication: Is There a System? Ann Arbor: Institute for Social Research, University of Michigan.

HAVELOCK, RONALD G. and DAVID A. LINGWOOD (1973) R & D Utilization Strategies and Functions: An Analytical Comparison of Four Systems. Ann Arbor: Institute for Social Research, University of Michigan.

JOLY, JEAN-MARIE (1967) "Research and innovation: two solitudes?" Canadian Education and Research Digest 2: 184-194.

KNEZO, GENEVIEVE J. (1974) Program Evaluation: Emerging Issues of Possible Legislative Concern Relating to the Conduct and Use of Evaluation in the Congress and the Executive Branch. Washington, DC: Congressional Research Service.

LIKERT, RENSIS and RONALD LIPPITT (1963) "The utilization of social science," in L. Festinger and D. Katz (eds.) Research Methods in the Behavioral Sciences. New York: Dryden.

LIPPITT, RONALD and RONALD HAVELOCK (1968) "Needed research on research utilization," in Research Implication for Educational Diffusion. East Lansing: Department of Education, Michigan State University.

LUNDBERG, CRAIG C. (1966) "Middlemen in science utilization: some notes toward clarifying conversion roles." American Behavioral Scientist 9 (February): 11-14.

National Science Foundation (1969) Knowledge into Action: Improving the Nation's Use of the Social Sciences. Report of the Special Commission of the National Science Board. Washington, DC: National Science Foundation.

PATTON, MICHAEL QUINN (1978) Utilization Focused Evaluation. Beverly Hills, CA: Sage.

ROBERTS, A. O. H. and J. K. LARSEN (1971) Effective Use of Mental Health

Research Information. AIR 820. Palo Alto, CA: American Institutes for Research.

ROGERS, EVERETT M. (1967) "Communication of vocational rehabilitation innovations," pp. 19-32 in Communication, Dissemination and Utilization of Rehabilitation Research Information. Studies in Rehabilitation Counselor Training No. 5. Washington, DC: Joint Liaison Committee of the Council of State Administrators of Vocational Rehabilitation and the Rehabilitation Counselor Educators, Department of Health, Education, and Welfare.

ROSENBLATT, AARON (1968) "The practitioner's use and evaluation of research." Social Work 13: 53-59.

ROTHMAN, JACK (1980) Social R & D: Research and Development in the Human Services. Englewood Cliffs, NJ: Prentice-Hall.

——— (1974) Planning and Organizing for Social Change: Action Principles from Social Science Research. New York: Columbia University Press.

SCANLON, JOHN and JOHN WALLER (1978) "Program evaluation and better federal programs." Presented at ASPA Conference, Phoenix.

SCHMUCK, RICHARD (1968) "Social psychological factors in knowledge utilization," pp. 143-173 in T. L. Eidell and J. M. Kitchel (eds.) Knowledge Production and Utilization in Educational Administration. Eugene: Center for the Advanced Study of Educational Administration, University of Oregon.

SCHWARTZ, DAVID C. (1966) "On the growing popularization of social science: the expanding public and problems of social science utilization. American Behavioral Scientist 9, 10: 47-50.

SHARPE, L. J. (1975) "The social scientist and policy-making: some cautionary thought and transatlantic reflections." Journal of Policy and Politics 4, 2: 7-34.

SHORT, E. C. (1973) "Knowledge production and utilization in curriculum: a special case of the general phenomenon." Review of Educational Research 43: 237-301.

SIEBER, S. D., K. S. LOUIS, and L. METZGER (1974) "The use of educational knowledge: evaluation of the pilot state dissemination program," in H. Hug (eds.) Evolution/Revolution: Library-Media-Information Futures. New York: Bowker.

SMITH, GILBERT (1972) "Research policy: 'pure' and 'applied'." British Hospital Journal and Social Science Review (April): 723-724.

WEISS, CAROL H. (1977) "What makes social research usable: data from mental health." Presented at the annual meeting of the American Association for the Advancement of Science, Denver.

WILSON, JAMES Q. (1978) "Social science and public policy: a personal note," in Laurence E. Lynn, Jr. (ed.) Knowledge and Policy: The Uncertain Connection. Washington, DC: National Academy of Sciences.

Chapter 2

STRUCTURAL FACTORS CONDUCIVE
TO RESEARCH UTILIZATION

Theoretical literature in sociology and in the area of organizational analysis, from Weber on, takes as a fundamental priniciple the importance of structural factors in affecting the behavior of organizations and the actors within them. It is evident that such structural elements may have a bearing on the manner in which research is processed and used within an organizational setting. In our field interviews, both agency directors and senior researchers recurrently referred to structural conditions that tended to facilitate or impede the application of internally generated information.

In an analysis of social services, Kogan (1963) concluded that failure to utilize findings resulted from overlooking organizational variables that determine utilization. Glaser' and Taylor (1969) reviewed successful and unsuccessful applied research projects in the field of mental health. Successful projects manifested high awareness of the organizational environment and the use of structural arrangements such as committees and formal and informal communication channels. Findings in various other studies point in a similar direction, as subsequent discussion will demonstrate.

This chapter on structural variables will be followed by one concerned with process variables. Structure and process, like anatomy and physiology, should be viewed as holistically related and integrated. For purposes of convenience in presentation, the two topics have been divided in the text. These chapters, however, should be seen as possessing substantive continuity and should be read from that perspective. Data from the interviews fell into five structural areas, which shall be discussed in turn: top-level support in the organizational system; structural access by researchers to applied personnel in planning and service delivery functions; specific structural forms and mechanisms associated with the research function; supportive forms and mechanisms in the broader organizational system; and the environmental context.

UTILIZATION OF RESEARCH IS FACILITATED BY TOP-LEVEL SUPPORT IN THE ORGANIZATIONAL SYSTEM

The Commitment and Support of the Chief Administrative Officer

Numerous comments by both agency managers and researchers pointed to the crucial role of the top administrator in creating conditions favorable to research utilization. Respondents, discussing positive utilization experiences in their situations, made the following typical observations:

> Successful research utilization is related to the director's personal views and attitudes. He appreciates the place and role of research and respects and gives feedback to researchers.
> The director is very supportive — 100%. He has been responsive and believes in objectivity, good data, good staff. I'd be dead without him.
> The director set up this research section as an extension of his own function and activity. He wants the department to be seen as an effective organization and sees research as a useful tool for this purpose.

What characteristics do directors possess that make them supportive of research? The director who holds a change-oriented attitude and has had positive experiences with research in the past seems to support research in his or her organization. Also, directors who are associated with external research organizations support research within their own organizations. Respondents described these aspects of director support as follows:

> The director is openminded and change-agent oriented. He aims for continual improvement in productivity. He tries to get this attitude and value set over to the staff — how can we do this job better? He has direct informal contact with staff, and tries to create a climate receptive to self-examination.
> The director must continually convince himself and other senior managers to relate research ideas to client needs. This should dominate — client service at the least cost.
> The director is chairman of the National Social Service Directors Research Committee. To him the truth has some value in an ideal way.
> The director had done collaborative work with the university research faculty in the past.

Research-oriented directors were said to possess a "willingness to be convinced by authentic research" combined with "interest in management-type information" and "client needs."

One researcher indicated a severe problem when the director was not supportive:

> I had a problem with the director — he is erratic and "political." I work around him by influencing all other members of the management team.

This same director gives his opinion of research:

> Research information is always only one sector — never a comprehensive view — but I am provoked by it. The ex-

ecutive must synthesize a comprehensive view, weaving many strands into a fabric of decision.

One researcher cautioned that, although directors should be supportive, they also should not be blindly accepting. The director must make judgments and maintain a broad view of the organization's activities:

> Managers should be very critical of their research people. They should ask, "what does the project mean for *this* community?"

A director may be supportive of research but not for the same reason as the researcher. One researcher commented that the director should ask of the researchers, "Help us understand," not "tell us what to do." This was a researcher who was knowledge oriented rather than operations-research oriented. In this case, our dual-interview procedure revealed that the director and researcher did not agree entirely on the function of research. In addition to administrative support, consistency regarding objectives on the part of the key actors is a relevant factor.

The views of the respondents are reflected in various places in the literature. Churchman (1964:37), for example, states that a research staff seeking to bring out a recommended change would be entirely thwarted unless "the manager pays attention to the problem." Wolfensberger (1969) writes about matters that administrators should consider in making decisions about supporting and using research within their agencies. He indicates that administrators need to explore their conscious and unconscious attitudes towards research; it is counterproductive for the administrator to think, "research, yes — but not here, now." With regard to background attributes of administrators, Cherns (1970) analyzed various case examples of successful utilization and concluded that a common feature was that the administrators, in these instances, had formerly been researchers themselves. Blum and Downing (1964) report that innovative use of new knowledge can take place, even in the face of active staff resistance, given that administrative support and sanctions are firm.

Legitimation at the Highest Level of Organizational Systems

Several respondents claimed that their efforts at research utilization were assisted by legitimation at the highest organizational levels, or that such efforts were impeded by the absence of legitimation.

Each agency in the study is governed by an elected council within the borough or county (like an American city council). The council has within its structure a committee for social services, and the director of the social service agency is appointed by the council. The council and chief borough officer (similar to a city administrator), then, are an important legitimating source for using research:

> The borough's commitment to forward planning is important, particularly the borough executive.
> The council, itself, emphasizes the need and use of research among its units as a basis for planning and allocation of funds. Members of the council urged it.
> The council members insist on evidence and programs based on evidence to gain authorization and funds. It is the only way to get resources in this country.

The social services committee also acts as a legitimating source when it requires certain information:

> The social services committee had to make a decision and was most desirous of having good information.
> The general public or community may provide legitimation. We are assisted by public concern over the issue. There was a

bandwagon effect, a favorable climate of opinion in the community.
Because monies were involved, it is necessary to be sure about what you are doing and to have proper public legitimation.

One research officer indicated that his work would be aided by the existence of a formalized policy statement making explicit the place and significance of research for the organization:

There are no short, specific, policy position statements that clarify the relationship of research to application. A description of how my staff and I are relevant to the department's needs does not exist. A professional document which clarifies and legitimates would help.
We should formalize research in official statements. This would provide more of a structure. A statement by the hierarchy, sanctioned and circulated by them, with meaningful job descriptions (which don't exist currently) would encourage more utilization.

This respondent felt that useful legitimating documents could emanate both from his professional association of researchers (giving professional rationale) and from top management in the agency (giving organizational sanction).

This same issue has been commented upon by a number of students of the field. Lippitt and Havelock (1968), for example, tell us that adopters or utilizers need to feel that their actions are legitimized so they are not unduly inhibited by fear of being judged. Gurel (1975:12) speaks of the importance of

the sponsoring authority which legitimates or authorizes or orders the provision of services. This can be a board of directors, Congress, a state legislature, the (now) Office of Management and Budget. . . . It would be a mistake to neglect the fact that these kinds of sanctioning bodies possess the real life and death power over both program services and their evaluation...and often do figure centrally in evaluation efforts.

The significance of top-level legitimation is underscored in this statement. In a review of case studies of organizational research, Glock (1961) found that research is most effectively used where the decision to use it is at the policy level, and interested management people carefully follow through.

The Function of Research Within the Organization, Explicitly Defined as Serving the Planning and Service Objectives of the Organization

A formally constituted *mission orientation* was said by many respondents to facilitate utilization of research products. A good proportion of respondents indicated the need for a clear policy that research basically serves the planning and operations objectives of the organization and is not a contemplative or knowledge-producing activity in its own right. Research, it was stated, should be structured to provide information for problem-solving within the unique context of a department providing social services:

> The research unit should limit its activity to specific problems related to department objectives and concerns.
> Use research as a practical tool, serving policy ends.
> Do studies that help save money and take pressures off the organization.

Broader, more substantial research undertaking should be carried out in conjunction with universities, according to one director. Several departments have attempted to institute this position by excluding the word "research" entirely from the title of the unit in which research is situated and to convey the emphasis of the unit by using titles such as "Development," "Planning," and "Coordination and Development."

I would make the point that "research" in local social service departments is not research in the traditional sense, but, instead, is aimed at aiding planning decisions. So it is specialized problem-solving, not geared to develop theory or to arrive at generalizations or to contribute to knowledge. Don't confuse the issue and give it more and different implications than it can claim. We call this section "Development" to avoid this confusion.

Appendix B presents an agency document reflecting this perspective.

If researchers know the problems of the organization, research is more likely to be produced to solve them:

Research staff should be in touch and have concern with practical issues. Our researcher was a child care worker and this has helped. He knew the problem.

Yet researchers may feel stagnated in this problem-solving role:

You must find the right balance between proper, responsible organizational accountability and freedom for researchers to demonstrate skills, creativity, and effectiveness in their professional area.

Others talk of the necessity for research to criticize and disturb the organization rather than to serve and placate it. Finding the proper tension between scholarly detachment and commitment to the organization is of critical importance.

The responses of respondents are given support in part by an empirical study by Van de Vall et al. (1976: 166) of industrial firms in the Netherlands. The objective of the study was to determine variables that were associated with use of applied research in management decisions. The investigators found that the more the research was internal and problem-specific to the organization, the more likely it was to be used.

In emphasizing this point they comment: "Instead of facilitating or stimulating the utilization of social research...formal sociological theory plays a *negative* role in the change process." Cherns (1967: 317-318) makes the point that a less agency-focused research department may find it easier to recruit and retain good research workers, but "from the standpoint of the organization as a whole, they might as well be on the other side of the moon."

UTILIZATION OF RESEARCH IS FACILITATED BY THE STRUCTURAL CONNECTION OF RESEARCHERS TO APPLIED PERSONNEL IN PLANNING AND SERVICE-DELIVERY FUNCTIONS

Structured Access of the Research Unit to the Top Planning Functions, to the Director, and to the Senior Management Team

Researchers were said often to lack association with planners. They either separated themselves from management or management kept them apart:

Researchers keep themselves out of the organization mainstream. They sit apart from management and the "tough decisions." They overly stress objectivity and aloofness.

One solution, according to several respondents, is to connect the research function structurally with the planning function. (This assumes the absence of a unified research and development or research and planning unit):

Position research within the organization so it is located closer to the director and management group.
Researchers should involve themselves in the planning function. Organizationally, researchers should have a say in planning.

To accomplish this, several suggestions were made:

> Management group meetings should include researchers. Also, managers should show directly the need and appreciation of their work.
> Our researcher is a member of the management team — a full member, right from the beginning, with a direct link to the management team and the committee.
> The researcher participates directly as a member of the management team, and is accountable for a number of management and planning functions.

One researcher, who had not been a member of the management team, worked himself into the group because he felt it was necessary. He persisted in making it known that there was a need to be involved if he was to be helpful. He became an official member although he was not originally structured in.

In addition to formal access to this group, researchers can make use of informal linkages. One researcher got along well informally with the director. She dealt with him directly. The deputy director, her superior, was neutral and did not get in the way.

Gurel (1975) takes the view that the main impediments to successful research utilization are not technical and methodological but are, rather, inherent in human and interpersonal strains between research staff and agency managers. These strains, according to Gurel, originate in different organizational perspectives of the two roles. The manager is largely concerned with stability and survival, the research person with innovation and change. According to this analysis, research staff need to associate more with managers in order to bring their own perspectives more in line with those engaged in planning and managing functions. In analyzing research functions in British social service departments, Benjamin (1972:26) advocates a close structural tie between research and managment:

It is much better...that a research unit should be attached to the Chief Executive Office (as part of his managerial equipment) than it should be placed in some committed department where inevitably it will find itself in a defensive political position.

Just as researchers need to be associated with processes of planning and managing, managers need to relate themselves to the tasks of researchers. In a study of a special National Opinion Research Center program designed to provide information to policy makers, Rich (1975: 244) concludes, "policy makers should be involved in the decision concerning what information to collect. They should continue to be involved in decisions concerning how the information is to be processed and used." Rich (1975: 245) goes on to call for

continuous feedback between policy makers and the staff providing information to them...Both researchers and policy makers will be more sensitive to each other's needs and ways of communicating if this type of contact is established.

Structured Access of the Research Unit to Field Operations People

A number of respondents indicated that research staff are aided in their work by having sanction to visit different branches of the organization and to become familiar with its everyday problems and activities. Thus, research people apparently need channels into the operational sphere and the realm of management and planning.

In professional organizations, especially those having somewhat decentralized or "human relations" structures, managers are not able to obtain compliance with planning decisions through fiat. A measure of autonomy and privacy is retained by professional staff members. Some changes in professional function within the organization can only be brought about by persuasion, discussion, and the influence of informal personal relationships. Thus, if research-originated plans developed at the administrative level are to be manifested in agency service operations, direct and ongoing contact between researchers and line staff may be necessary. This was suggested recurrently in the field interviews.

As stated earlier, researchers are sometimes viewed as being "aloof" by both management and operations staff:

> There are tense attitudes between those who deal with immediate operations and research people who are protected. Researchers don't have enough and need more access to various staff groups.

It was felt that operational staff may develop a favorable research attitude if they see that research is directly meeting their needs:

> Develop a climate in which research information is seen as relevant. Relationships of researchers and service staff need to be closer. Such staff have to feel that their needs are the concern of the research and that research is a resource they can use.
> There needs to be confidence of staff in the research section — that it is dealing with real issues, that it is not only senior management oriented but also staff and program oriented.
> Researchers must maintain their credibility with staff — recognize the social worker's tasks and situation and help him with his immediate practice problems.

It was felt that if research findings are carefully fed back to operational staff as an aid to improving their task performance, they will value research more:

> Follow up with staff in terms of spelling out the implications of findings, such as redoing assessment forms to bring them more in line with research implications.

One department employed the concept of flexible, indistinct boundaries between the research unit and operational units to achieve interaction:

> The boundary between R & D and operations is unclear and overlapping. This creates tension and uncertainty, but this is good because we are forced to work things out together.

This arrangement led to occasional disputes and tensions, but the respondent felt that these were necessary and served a creative purpose.

In one agency the solution to aloofness of the researchers from the line staff was to place the research unit "in the middle of the organization" physically or geographically and psychologically. The unit was located away from the director's office and in proximity to program affairs and the main meeting and socializing rooms used by all staff:

> Research is often too much a headquarters-located operation, too removed from practitioners. Therefore, research is seen as parasitic, not dealing with real and important problems of the agency. We overcame this by putting research in the midst of the organization — not at the top (a management tool and captive) or outside (aloof, academic, technical).

The research unit enhanced its "middle" position by playing an overall communication role (putting out the agency newsletter) and performing unique service functions for the staff (taking responsibility for arrangements for some special events and social occasions). While these roles cut into time available for research tasks, the members of the unit felt that the benefits gained in application productivity greatly outweighed the detriments.

Brown (1976:2-3) places interpersonal contact and association in the context of linkage. This is described in the following way:

> Practitioners are not knowledgeable about research and modify their programs based on conversations with other practitioners.... . Researchers tend to do research of little interest to practitioners and practitioners continue to run programs with disproved or unproved methods. Linkage, however, between these two has been shown to improve relevancy of research and produce programs incorporating methods of proven merit.... . Linkage involves both formal and informal contact.

Specific evidence is available elsewhere in support of these contentions. For example, in Shartle's study (1961) of an occupational research program, it was concluded that research was utilized to a greater extent when research staff developed informal relationships with operational staff and when technical people were filtered into operating offices. Similarly, in Glock's (1961) comprehensive analysis of the Bureau of Applied Social Research program, cases of more successful utilization involved research units that were most highly integrated into operations.

UTILIZATION OF RESEARCH IS FACILITATED BY SPECIFIC STRUCTURAL FORMS AND MECHANISMS

The Existence of a Specialized Unit Within the Organization, Having the Joint Purpose of Research and Application

In our interviews participants recurrently spoke of a "lack of connection between planning and research." Several of them indicated that this connection was assisted by establishing a structure that combined both functions within a single unit:

> A C & D unit helped us. The existence of a research and implementing apparatus kept things moving.
> It has aided us to have a research and development unit.

The Coordinating and Development Unit (C & D) or the Research and Development Unit (R & D) provide a structural mechanism with the function and responsibility of both determining appropriate research and relating it organically to policy and operational aspects of the organization's work:

> A C & D unit, or something like that, is important. This unit can catch research, evaluate it, and develop forward motion. It provides machinery to make decisions and carry them out. Structure was important — planning and research as a separate combined unit — management and research tied together. You need to plug research directly into planning. Research is associated with planning directly in one manager, and he is senior — directly related to planning and policy at the highest level.
>
> Do some research and some planning yourself. Have a function that joins both.

One important consideration regarding the unit is the head person. The wrong individual can inhibit the right structure:

> I have no direct tie to the director or the senior planning group. The director works through his division (R & D). But the head man has not got his roots in research — he's not especially interested.

One of the foremost works in the study of innovations advocates the employment of a structure such as that suggested by the respondents (Rogers and Shoemaker, 1971: 314). In order to stimulate use of new ideas in an organization, one should "create an adaptive unit as part of the organization's structure. It may be called a research and development unit or some other euphemistic title." Based on available empirical evidence, Rothman (1974: 474) indicates: "Research conducted in mixed or applied settings is more likely to be both innovative and implemented."

In a study of a twenty-year occupational research program,

the investigator concludes that research was most frequently used when the research unit was also given responsibility for development and application (Shartle, 1961). A rationale for this is suggested by Churchman (1964: 34) as a result of examining deficiencies of the more traditional divided structural arrangement:

> One could say that the difficulty is that the available information is in one location. . . the analysis is in a second. . . and the decision-making in a third. One might feel that if all three of these components could be combined into one unit, the problem could be solved. This suggestion is a reasonable one.

Tropman (1978: 12) in reviewing policy planning for human services in the state of Wisconsin, proposes a consolidated planning and research unit that also includes budgeting responsibilities:

> In the highly complex organizations that are responsible for the delivery of human services, the development of policy must be viewed as a distinct organizational task. Ideally, this should take the form of central-level staff units which report directly to the chief administrative/policy-making officer of the department. It is essential that this unit have integrated inside itself primary functional specialties in the areas of planning, budgeting and evaluation so as to ensure the maximum impact of each of these policy-making disciplines and perspectives on critical policy decision.

Obviously, a structural device such as this is not, in and of itself, a panacea. For example, the actors within it used to be able to develop productive working relationships. But it does appear to be one potential means, in conjunction with others, of enhancing utilization.

The Existence of Various Specific Mechanisms That Link Research with Applied Tasks and Operational People

Respondents indicated that research utilization is facilitated by the existence of formally instituted mechanisms that specifically link research products to implementation and operational tasks. The need for personnel access and contact was previously stated. There is also a need for concrete means and mechanisms to accomplish this. These mechanisms involve roles, groups, meetings, and the like, that are built into the organizational superstructure. Some approaches to this in the departments studied include:

Development Officers Within Specialized Units

The presence of someone like the researcher — a senior person and a member of the management group, but not responsible for regular program tasks — is free to take on delegated director functions and be an extension of the director — to develop and monitor policies and engage in trouble shooting around research applications.

Development is the prescription of how policy is to be carried out. A development officer was useful to prescribe procedures to follow as agreed — as a line responsibility. The development officer here dealt not only in research application but also sees that these are related to the broader policy and political situation.

Development Panels, Project Teams, and Working Parties — All Composed of Mixed Research and Operational Personnel

Development panels in the department cut across branches on common interests.

The group around the research director put energy behind it — steered it through, leaned on program people, and kept them informed.

Management Teams Having Appropriate Mixed Membership

Researchers should be included in the management team — get researchers into the senior social workers group. Discussed reports formally at management team meeting, at assistant directors' meetings, and made decisions and set deadlines for pieces of implementation and set up implementation working groups. We kept the spotlight on this project.

Research Liaison Group

There is a research liaison group — a member of each unit of the department and the research team is included. It meets regularly, once a quarter, as a formal communication link.

Research liaison group — bimonthly meeting; information-sharing group with representatives from various units. People can demand research and evaluate it, suggest, and make criticisms in progress.

Research Activities Seminar

The New Projects Seminar meets once a month. It is staffed by the research and planning department. It is a way of looking at gaps, seeing what is being done, and what is left to do. It initiates new programs in new research projects.

We hold seminars that are separated from normal agency pressures. These are in a more open and relaxed climate. It gives us a chance to think reflectively about what to do with things coming at us from the research section.

These mechanisms will be discussed in greater detail as aspects of process in the next chapter.

The need for means of linkage between researchers and operational people is given high saliency in the literature. Brown (1976: 2) defines linkage as the "degree of connectiveness that exists among groups." He goes on to say that it can be measured by

the number, variety and mutuality of contacts and the degree to which they share collaborative relationships. The more linkages and the stronger they are, the more effective contacts will be and the greater the impact one system will have on the other.... . Research in a high linkage situation will develop to more closely meet user needs and will be more readily accepted.

Various mechanisms of linkage have been suggested. Davis and Salasin (1975) report on a "Problem-Solving Dialogue

Model," involving multiple linkages through an organization. Schwartz (1966) describes a "populizer role" that has a relationship to the development officers described by the respondents. Havelock (1968) delineates eight different types of linking roles and suggests that they may be sequenced in particular ways for maximum effect. While Schwartz recommends that social scientists be given specialized training in order to perform linking roles, Rogers (1967) suggests that practitioners be prepared to enact such tasks through pre-service or in-service training. It can be assumed that either approach could be usefully applied and additional experimentation with both should be encouraged.

Structured Balanced Competency
Within the Research Unit

It was stated by several respondents that the research unit should be made up of personnel with combined competence in research (design, statistical analysis, computer technology) and in application or operations (knowledge of planning process, of services, of social change, and of the functioning of the organization).

Some respondents felt that if a researcher was once a practitioner or a manager, relating research to application would be facilitated:

> People doing research should also have been practitioners. One research officer was a community worker — a chief social worker and health community worker. He is aggressive around the organization — knows when to get things moving. He didn't have research qualifications, but picked them up along the way.

The individual who heads the research unit apparently can be a researcher or an application person in terms of primary identity. One director says it depends upon who is available for the position. Another director comments that researchers "may be more threatening to top managers; a practitioner is safer, more predictable. He is a more comfortable and familiar figure." A different director states that the head of the unit should "embrace both functions."

It was felt that at the field staff level multiple perspectives were also necessary:

> Researchers must be knowledgeable at a very specific operational level. This means the researcher is also capable and committed to research. He won't weaken that, but temper it by application relevance.

One research officer said he already had five researchers on his staff and that in expanding, he would prefer to hire two individuals with planning skills for the research unit. This would give the unit balance and enhance application potentialities.

Selection procedures were said to be important in acquiring combined competencies:

> We need a better selection procedure to get qualified, experienced people. Take into account their applied interests and abilities to participate in department processes. The person must see things through. Lack of experience in planning on the part of research people is a detriment.

The composite characteristics and skills needed by planning-development personnel were listed by one respondent:

> research comprehension, experience, or skill — operational comprehension, experience, or skill — ability to integrate differing ideas and tendencies — ability to deal organizationally — a personality that is assertive and moves ahead against organizational obstacles.

In summary, various respondents felt strongly that research unit staff, individually or in aggregate, need combined competence in application and development as well as research skills.

These results of field interviews are substantiated in various places in the literature. Havelock (1969), for example, states that in order to obtain adequate "throughput" of knowledge utilization, there is a need for a newer style of leadership that includes a *mix* of technical, organizational, and human relations skills. Another type of skill balance is indicated by Benjamin (1972). Speaking specifically of the British social services setting, he describes the following set of skills as necessary in the research-utilization context: data collector and designer, data analyst, subject matter specialist, and result producer (an expert in report presentation, report writing, and advising operational staff about applications). The need for mixed competencies is explained by Mackie and Christensen (1967): "Formulation of possible applications of research findings requires extensive knowledge of the field of application in which the research is to be attempted." Researchers are often too casual about the degree to which they need to be intimately familiar with the context of utilization. Sometimes such specialized familiarity is not reasonable to expect from the technical researcher. It is, therefore, possibly useful to think of the applied research task as comprising a system made up of varied but interrelated interests and capabilities.

In addition to the areas already discussed, a smaller number of comments were made regarding certain other necessary attributes and functions of the research unit. These will be summarized briefly, without elaboration.

Size of the Research Unit

Respondents felt that the research unit should be of sufficient size to make it "viable." There should be an ample number of research staff and sufficient clerical support. Size was related to flexibility, maneuverability, and having the capacity "to be responsive."

Keep regular projects going and respond to short-time projects also. Leave room for short-term activities to be responsive. We need enough staff for both.

The comments of respondents did not place the size factor in the context of "empire building." Concern over utilization logically requires a substantial increment in energy and skill in guiding this process, beyond that required for the technical tasks of conducting studies.

Continuity of Staff Within the Research Unit

It was reported to be helpful if the unit has a reasonable degree of longevity and continuity among its staff. According to respondents, this facilitates working relationships within the unit and with operational staff and managers outside it. Social relations that are developed over time aid professional roles related to the research function:

Familiarity and interpersonal contact helps. I know most of the people on the social work side because I worked here for a long time.

Research staff are directly related to the line-area workers. This is facilitated by the senior researcher being a qualified social worker, being there a long time, and knowing many of the area people for many years.

Continuity of research people facilitates relationships; this enables us to connect previous work to current projects.

Continuity of staff permits relating new projects to those already completed. This means that there is also continuity from one project to another.

The Existence of Organizational Integrative Tasks on the Part of the Research Unit

Certain integrative tasks on the part of the unit, not of a strictly research character, were said to facilitate interrelationships with staff. This may be related to the "middle of the organization" response, dealing with issuing a general information newsletter, taking responsibility for social events, and so on.

UTILIZATION OF RESEARCH IS FACILITATED BY SUPPORTIVE FORMS AND MECHANISMS WITHIN THE BROADER ORGANIZATIONAL SYSTEM

While most of the comments made in the interviews focused specifically on the research task and the research unit, a fewer number indicated that features of the larger organizational system can have a bearing on utilization. These will be reported upon briefly and without elaboration. The more limited treatment does not imply that less importance should be attached to these items in an overall assessment of research utilization.

The Existence of Time Within the Organization To Reflect and Act on Research Information

Respondents frequently cited time as an important inhibiting or facilitative factor in digesting and using research. There are "pressures to ameliorate immediate problems," and "other competing demands are stronger." It was recommended that time should be set aside within the normal work assignments of field operations and management staff to digest and apply research findings. Too often this is an unplanned, hit-or-miss kind of activity that is set aside whenever more "important" or "pressing" operational problems appear.

The Existence Generally of Effective Communication Channels Within the Organization

Norms that support good communication and functioning communication networks were spoken for. Generally good communication within the organization can enhance communication of research specifically. It serves to encourage the circulation of research information, leads to greater attention to reports, and thus acts as an aid to utilization.

One particular structural element mentioned was the nature of the hierarchy within the organization. A flat hierarchy was said to allow circulation and communication of information. It was stated that a flat hierarchy "opens communication throughout the department" so that research information can readily reach the relevant people.

The Existence of High-Quality Operational Staff Within the Organization

Several respondents felt that research activities are enhanced by the existence in the organization of a large number of high-quality operational professional staff who are committed to professional goals and are not satisfied to function as "mere technicians."

> There are many high-quality professional staff in this agency. We're committed to recognizing the academic content of the profession, not just seeing researchers and practitioners as technicians. Such staff push forward the boundaries of knowledge, examine their premises. The corpus of knowledge is not closed in their view. This encourages examination of research as a source for growth and enhancement of the profession.

In addition to operational staff of high quality, it was stated that managers need to be trained to work with numbers:

> Managers can't interpret basic statistics. They're not comfortable with figures. They need training in statistical areas.

The Presence of Specialist Roles in the Organization Other Than Research

It was suggested by several respondents that the existence of certain types of specialist roles, in addition to those located in a research and application unit, foster the ingathering of research information from outside the organization. These roles include subject matter specialists in areas such as child welfare, aging, or physical rehabilitation, and staff with responsibilities in the area of training and staff development. Such individuals are particularly eager to receive new information pertaining to their specialty. They appear more likely both to seek such information outside the organization and to pay attention to information developed within.

UTILIZATION OF RESEARCH IS FACILITATED BY SUPPORT IN THE ENVIRONMENTAL SYSTEM SURROUNDING THE UTILIZING ORGANIZATION

While most of the comments by respondents dealt with factors internal to the organization, a considerable number of observations noted the significance of the environmental context in which the organization was located. Certain specific elements of the environment were pointed to as important.

The Climate of Public Opinion in the Community

One director indicated that public opinion had helped decide a utilization issue:

> There was public concern over this issue. A community consensus built up and members of the council felt that they had to go along with the climate of opinion.

It was pointed out by one respondent that, when research favors certain types of clients that have appeal to the general public, this facilitates utilization. For example, neglected children or the handicapped have popular support, whereas delinquents or multiproblem families do not.

A researcher indicated that the agency service area comprised a university town. There exists a highly educated constituency, sympathetic to rationality and careful planning in community decision-making. This has aided the research function. Another respondent gave a similar but counterposed comment:

> Planning must take into account local identity and the uniqueness of the community. Our situation is one in which a conservative viewpoint prevails. This places a limit on the amount of public expenditure we can depend upon for social programs. And what we do request must be strongly rationalized from a research point of view.

In the literature it has been pointed out by Paisley (1969) that transfer of knowledge is associated with the cultural climate in which transfer takes place. Values and traditions, he states, critically impact upon the knowledge-transfer process. Glaser (1973) makes the point that successful utilization requires a sensitivity to the context, including the organizational framework and the character of public opinion.

Political Climate

Respondents recurrently referred to the importance of political backing in the community in order to acquire the legitimation and resources necessary to implement programs:

> Our report on the need for services for the under-five age group went through quickly. The local council has a strong Labour majority and the national party manifesto has stressed this as a priority item.
> Our community is very political. The counselors are generally conservative. The research program has had to take a low profile. Not only don't they support research recommenda-

tions about services, they also have insisted that we cut back on the amount of research that we do.

Certain community groups in particular exert powerful political influence:

Our report on changing the meals-on-wheels program ran into strong opposition. The unions objected to the increased workload that would result.

The effects of politics on research efforts is widely recognized. Weiss (1977: 14) points out that operations research or program evaluation often serves as "political ammunition" to "neutralize opponents, convince waverers, and bolster supporters." Caplan et al. (1975: 49) make the point even more strongly in the following passage:

Political implications of research findings appear to override any other consideration in determining utilization. Social science data are rarely of such compelling force as to take precedence over their political significance, not only with respect to the use of data, but with respect to the deliberate nonuse as well. Most respondents shared the belief that social scientists were naive about policy-making and the role of politics in determining the utility of their research findings.

Economic Resources

The availability of resources to carry forward the implications of research is a key element in utilization. Among resources, those of an economic nature are, perhaps, most crucial. This was brought home in numerous interviews. On the negative side:

The study was rejected because the economic situation had deteriorated and the council would not approve the funds. There are stringent economic restrictions in dealing with recommendations for new services. We have to deal with financial priorities and be aware of economic feasibility.

And on the positive side:

> Our situation has been favorable to implementation of research findings. We have a rich community and a liberal council that is sympathetic to provision of social services.

The sheer size of the human services enterprise is a factor:

> Our department is large and has a great number of functions. Because considerable amounts of money are involved, we have to be attuned to the economic realities and be sure of the basis for our recommendations.

The importance of economic considerations has been underlined by Donnison (1972: 521):

> Research workers who apply their minds to problems of public policy and government must be aware of economic and social changes and the trends of policy and opinion in their field.

It has been brought out by Paisley (1969) that the economic system influences the basic quality and quantity of research information in circulation through the pattern of research funding.

Other External Factors

Among other external influences that were cited were the following three:

Professional Associations and "Invisible Colleges" of Colleagues

> The director takes part in research support groups. He is a member of a committee on research of the association of directors.

Research Institutes and Universities

Schools and research institutes in the community have expressed an interest in our research, and this has influenced the director and other senior staff members to more highly value the importance of the research that has been conducted.

Multiple Inputs and Pressures from the Outside

We are impeded by the volume of influences acting upon us. There is an overload of information and a need to sort out the impact of the multiplicity of policies and interacting agencies and organizations that surround us.

A useful perspective for acknowledging and dealing with the environmental context has been given by Davis and Salasin (1975):

> The wise change consultant often will advise delaying the implementation of an idea until events occur which will increase the probability of adoption. Some common events having that effect include the arrival of a new leader, a new budget cycle, crises, new legislation, the availability of exciting and challenging practice techniques, mounting dissatisfaction with conditions, and even seasonal variations.

AN APPLICATION CHECKLIST FOR STRUCTURAL FACTORS

As a way of summarizing and indicating the implications of the results of the interviews, a checklist of variables identified by respondents is presented below. The results of the field interviews are viewed as hypotheses rather than definitive propositions because of the exploratory nature of the study. That these factors have received additional empirical and/or theoretical support in the relevant literature suggests that they merit serious consideration. The checklist, while still a tentative set of variables, is given in this format for convenience to the reader in reviewing the material and as an aid to thinking about its potential utilization as judged appropriate in given agency circumstances.

Hierarchical Support and Legitimation

- ☐ Does the chief administrative officer support the research function?
- ☐ Does the top policy board sanction and support research?
- ☐ Is there an official statement by the organization explicitly sanctioning research and defining it as serving the planning/service objectives of the organization?

Structural Connections Between Research and Operations

- ☐ Can researchers move around in the environment of operations?
- ☐ Are there opportunities within the structure for informal contacts between researchers and planners/administrators?
- ☐ Do researchers have access to administrative planning, and are they given an active role in this process?
- ☐ Are researchers located in reasonable physical proximity to planners and administrators?[1]
- ☐ Is there access by researchers to service personnel?
- ☐ Are researchers located in reasonable physical proximity to service personnel?[2]
- ☐ Does the research unit perform some organizationally integrative functions that are not of a strict research nature?

Specific Structural Forms and Mechanisms

- ☐ Does a specialized unit exist within the organization that has a joint research and application function?

Do specific linking mechanisms exist, such as:

- ☐ development officers?
- ☐ development panels, project teams, and working parties composed of mixed research and operations personnel?
- ☐ research liaison groups representing different units and functions?
- ☐ research study groups or seminars?

Is there balanced competency in the research unit with respect to:
- [ ] technical research competency?
- [ ] competency in pertinent operational areas?
- [ ] sensitivity to organizational and interpersonal dynamics?
- [ ] resolve and skill in moving ahead in the face of organizational obstacles?
- [ ] ability to integrate diverse ideas and tendencies, theoretical and applied?

Supportive Forms and Mechanisms in the Broader Organizational System

- [ ] Is there a sufficient allocation of time within the organization to reflect and act on research information?
- [ ] Are there generally effective communication channels within the organization?
- [ ] Is the service staff composed of high-quality professionals in terms of training and professional motivation?
- [ ] Are there an ample number of specialists who are experts in delimited subject areas?

Support in the External Environmental System

- [ ] Is there a favorable climate of public opinion within the community for research-relevant activities?
- [ ] Does the organization attempt to cultivate such attitudes?
- [ ] Is there a favorable political climate for research-relevant activities?
- [ ] Does the organization attempt to cultivate such attitudes?
- [ ] Are there economic resources in the community sufficient to support programmatic implications of research?
- [ ] Do research undertakings and recommendations take account of the resource base?

- ☐ Do community professional associations and research institutes add support to the research function?
- ☐ Is an attempt made to maximize such support potentialities?

These, then, are the principal structural factors that were identified. Our attention will now shift to the dynamic aspect of structure. In the next chapter we will concentrate on processes and procedures that operate within and between structures and that may be said to constitute the physiology of linkage. What now follows should be viewed as an extension of this discussion of structures, rather than as entirely new subject matter.

NOTES

1. Proximity to both administrators and service staff may be difficult. Both types of proximity were said to be useful. It might be possible to emphasize one or the other proximity, locate the research office between both groups, or decentralize the research staff in both locations.

2. See note 1.

REFERENCES

BENJAMIN, BERNHARD (1972) "Research strategies in social service departments of local authorities in Great Britain." Journal of Social Policy 2, 1: 13-26.

BLUM, R. H. and J. J. DOWNING (1964) "Staff responses to innovation in a mental health service." American Journal of Public Health 54: 1230-1240.

BROWN, TIMOTHY (1976) "Guidelines for integrating program evaluation with administrative decision making." Presented at APA Convention, Washington, DC.

CAPLAN, NATHAN, A. MORRISON, and R. STAMBAUGH (1975) The Use of Social Science Knowledge in Policy Decisions at the National Level: A Report to Respondents. Ann Arbor: Institute for Social Research, University of Michigan.

CHERNS, ALBERT B. (1970) "Relations between research institutions and users of research." International Social Science Journal 22, 2: 226-242.

――― (1967) "The use of the social sciences." Human Relations: 313-325.

CHURCHMAN, C. WEST (1964) "Managerial acceptance of scientific recommendations." California Management Review 7, 1: 31-38.

DAVIS, HOWARD and SUSAN SALASIN (1975) "The utilization of evaluation," ppl. 621-666 in Elmer Struening and Marcia Guttentag (eds.) Handbook of Evaluation Research, Vol. 1. Beverly Hills, CA: Sage.

DONNISON, DAVID (1972) "Research for policy." Minerva 10, 4: 519-536.

GLASER, EDWARD M. (1973) "Knowledge transfer and institutional change." Professional Psychology 4: 434-444.

――― and S. TAYLOR (1969) Factors Influencing the Success of Applied Research. Washington, DC: National Institute of Mental Health, Department of Health, Education, and Welfare.

GLOCK, CHARLES Y. (1961) "Applied social research: some conditions affecting its utilization," pp. 1-19 in Case Studies in Bringing Behavioral Science into Use: Studies in the Utilization of Behavioral Science, Vol. 1. Palo Alto, CA; Institute for Communication Research, Stanford University.

GUREL, LEE (1975) "The human side of evaluating human services programs," pp. 11-28 in Marcia Guttentag and Elmer Struening (eds) Handbook of Evaluation Research, Vol. 2. Beverly Hills, CA: Sage.

HAVELOCK, RONALD G. (1969) Planning for Innovation through Dissemination and Utilization of Knowledge. Ann Arbor: Center for Research on Utilization of Scientific Knowledge, Institute for Social Research, University of Michigan.

――― (1968) "Dissemination and translation roles," pp. 64-119 in T. L. Eidell and J. M. Kitchel (eds.) Knowledge Production in Educational Administration. Eugene: Center for the Advanced Study of Educational Administration, University of Oregon.

KOGAN, L. S. (1963) "The utilization of social work research." Social Casework 44: 569-574.

LIPPITT, RONALD and RONALD HAVELOCK (1968) "Needed research on research utilization," in Research Implication for Educational Diffusion. East Lansing: Department of Education, Michigan State University.

MACKIE, R. R. and P. R. CHRISTENSEN (1967) Translation and Application of Psychological Research. Technical Report 716-1. Goleta, CA: Santa Barbara Research Park, Human Factors Research.

PAISLEY, WILLIAM J. (1969) "Perspectives on the utilization of knowledge." Presented at the meeting of the American Educational Research Association, Los Angeles, February.

RICH, ROBERT F. (1975) "Selective utilization of social science related information by federal policy-makers." Inquiry 13, 3: 239-245.

ROGERS, EVERETT M. (1967) "Communication of vocational rehabilitation innovations," pp. 19-32 in Communication, Dissemination and Utilization of Rehabilitation Research Information. Studies in Rehabilitation Counselor Training No. 5. Washington, DC: Joint Liaison Committee of the Council of State Administrators of Vocational Rehabilitation and Rehabilitation Counselor Educators, Department of Health, Education, and Welfare.

——— and F. F. SHOEMAKER (1971) Communication of Innovations: A Cross-Cultural Approach. New York: Macmillan.

ROTHMAN, JACK (1974) Planning and Organizing for Social Change: Action Principles from Social Science Research. New York: Columbia University Press.

SHARTLE, CARROLL L. (1961) "The occupational research program: an example of research utilization," pp. 59-72 in Case Studies in Bringing Behavioral Science into Use: Studies in the Utilization of Behavioral Science, Vol. 1. Palo Alto, CA: Institute for Communication Research, Stanford University.

SCHWARTZ, DAVID C. (1966) "On the growing popularization of social science: the expanding public and problems of social science utilization." American Behavioral Scientist 9, 10: 47-50.

TROPMAN, PETER J. (1978) "Evaluation, policy making and budgeting: starting from scratch in Wisconsin." Delivered at the National Conference on the Future of Social Work Research, sponsored by the National Association of Social Workers, San Antonio, October.

VAN de VALL, MARK, CHERYL BOLAS and TAI S. KANG (1976) "Applied social research in industrial organizations: an evaluation of functions, theory, and methods." Journal of Applied Behavioral Science 12, 2: 158-177.

WEISS, CAROL H. (1977) "Introduction," in Carol H. Weiss (ed.) Using Social Research in Public Policy Making. Lexington, MA: D. C. Heath.

WOLFENSBERGER, WOLF (1969) "Dilemmas of research in human management agencies." Rehabilitation Literature (June): 162-169.

Chapter 3

THE RESEARCH PROCESS
AND RESEARCH UTILIZATION

Program evaluation and operations research embody a sociotechnical process. This entails a technical research methodology in interaction with human participants seeking attainment of certain social goals. The technical and social components are interlocked in a dynamic flow of actions (the process) resulting in a desired end product. It is important to be clear about the nature of the product. Sometimes this is visualized as information or data. Such a view is truncated and misleading. The end product of operations research, conducted in an organizational setting, is practical and behavioral—new services or policies, more effective delivery of current services, the elimination of unnecessary services, and greater efficiency in the administrative operation of the organization. Alternatively, we may view the process as involving the creation of information items or data that are actively used by organizational actors in agency operations to enhance organizational functioning. Because information, and its employment, must ideally be joined, it is best to consider this as a sociotechnical endeavor defined in process terms.

We may also approach the subject through the linkage concept introduced earlier. Linkage requires a connecting of research tasks and operational tasks, of research personnel and operational staff. Structural linkage, already discussed, is one way of accomplishing this. In and of itself, however, structure may be sterile and static if not articulated with appropriate implemental processes. Process involves the intermingling of the dual set of tasks and persons in collaborative sequences of action. These sequences of action are the arena in which the research-and-operations amalgam is worked through and consummated.

Many of the respondents placed emphasis on the importance of process. Two examples are particularly illuminating. The first describes the psychological aspect of process:

> Sometimes the process of research is as important as the findings themselves. It frees up thinking and focuses attention and interest on the issues being studied.

The second identifies political and strategic aspects:

> First of all, we started with a problem about which there was an awareness and interest — child care. We involved people, even though that took a long time. We interviewed pertinent field staff, talking with them about methods, problems, and findings. The research staff identified the people who would make or break the report among the field staff and supervisors. We also talked to the management people and kept them informed through reports.

This process orientation was underlined also by a National Institute of Mental Health supported study team that examined the matter of how to enhance research conducted in human service agency settings (Twain et al., 1974: 80). They conclude:

> Research is more likely to be utilized if administrators and practitioners are intimately involved in carrying out the pro-

gram, if staff are well versed in the research strategy, and if all the participants and interested groups and individuals are consulted and kept informed at every step of the way.

Based upon a review of responses by informants in the study, five steps seem to emerge as basic dimensions of process. These include:

(1) Defining the problem
(2) Carrying out the research
(3) Making recommendations
(4) Disseminating information and recommendations
(5) Engaging in development activities.

A dominant theme was that there should be vital participation by relevant agency actors at each of these steps. Participation may involve different configurations of actors at each step. The general point concerning participation was stated as follows:

Staff and other members of the agency have to feel that their needs are the concern of researchers and that research is a resource that is of use to them. You have to develop a climate in which research is seen as relevant. An important way to do this is to have people take part in research activities.

As will be seen, this theme is highlighted in a variety of different ways.

UTILIZATION OF RESEARCH IS FACILITATED WHEN RELEVANT OPERATIONAL PEOPLE PARTICIPATE IN DEFINING THE RESEARCH PROBLEM

There was considerable agreement that research was more likely to be dealt with seriously when it was based on needs identified by operational people within the organization. Respondents singled out a variety of different organizational groups that ought to participate in problem definition.

(1) *Field Staff* — Field people should be asked to take part in planning the research. This can be done in several different ways. We have used consultative committees. They help decide what kind of research to have.

(2) *Management* — Researchers should consult early on with management. They have to be aware of the concerns of management and of their obligation to meet research needs as seen by managers. Research should not be based only on the concerns of researchers, themselves.

(3) *Middle-Level Personnel* — Middle-level staff really know agency problems well. They can be very helpful in sharpening the problems to be looked into.

It was not a consensus of the respondents that any one of these agency constituencies should necessarily have a determining voice. For example, one suggestion was to have "working parties" made up of various levels of the organization, functioning on a team basis. Another view was to consult with various of these groups separately and serially as a way of formulating a comprehensive and balanced problem definition. Also, respondents frequently mentioned the importance of involving other significant people in the environment of the organization — political figures, community representatives, and government officials at higher levels.

"Listening" was described as a critical skill for researchers. When consulting with various groups, researchers have to know how to identify the needs that are being expressed:

The research team has to earn their license by getting in with staff, really listening to what people have to say, and showing that they are there to help. Field people know what is going on on the line. Researchers can pick up a lot of clues by paying attention to what they have to say.

At the same time, there was recognition that operational

people, including managers, often do not know how to ask proper research questions. Problems arise, it was stated, because people have asked the wrong questions or poorly articulated questions. Or they change the question in midstream, requiring researchers to go back to the beginning in conducting an inquiry. For this reason, listening was seen as having an active rather than a passive character. Researchers were asked to help those with whom they were working to come to a useful expression of their problem. This was to be done by "being very concise in posing issues," so that appropriately bounded inquiries could be undertaken. One respondent referred to the researcher as performing an "intermediary" role in assisting agency personnel to scale down questions from the overly broad perspective they usually bring.

The importance of the problem-definition stage has been well documented in the literature. Havelock and Lingwood (1973) conclude that after linkage, adequate diagnosis of real user need is the second most important element in research utilization. In reviewing research utilization in the rehabilitation field, Engstrom (1970) states that a critical factor is the existence of mutually defined and accepted objectives that can gain the commitment of the relevant parties. It is the view of Likert and Lippitt (1963) that being oriented to action problems, as perceived by operational people, permits the researcher to select the most appropriate scientific resources to apply to the solution of an organizational concern. Difficulties that operational people have in formulating their problems in research terms are brought out by Mackie and Christensen (1967) and these authors call for specially trained research personnel who have the willingness and capacity to assist with this task.

While both empirical and theoretical writings point to the salutary effects of conjoint problem definition on research utilization, Smith (1972) identifies a pitfall in this procedure.

He maintains that research studies so undertaken will be confined to topics on which a relatively high degree of consensus can be reached in the organization. This means that certain problems related to needed improvements in organizational functioning may be overlooked or bypassed. Feasibility and follow-through are given preference over some other objectives or values that are also important.

UTILIZATION OF RESEARCH IS FACILITATED WHEN RELEVANT OPERATIONAL PEOPLE PARTICIPATE IN CARRYING OUT THE RESEARCH

Operational staff can assist in a meaningful way in supporting the conduct of the study proper. This can take several forms. Planning the data-gathering phase is one of them:

> We involved staff members in planning forms, setting the time schedule, etc. They were with us at every stage.

Support may also be provided in administering data-gathering:

> After the general design of the study is completed, it's turned over to an information working party for further processing. This working party is made up of research people, an administrator, and practitioners. It is a mixed group. It sees that reports are submitted by staff and is responsible for monitoring the data-gathering phase.

Operational staff may be supportive by encouraging forms completion:

> A staff group was involved in motivating other staff to provide information. We were also active in helping to explain to staff why certain forms were necessary and how to fill them out.

Interpreting the data is yet another way operational staff can assist in the conduct of research:

> I was active in working with involved staff members in clarifying and interpreting what we were coming up with.

Through this arrangement, operational people aid in the development of procedures that are viable in the practice situation. Having conviction about this, they are in a position to motivate or pressure other operational people to comply with what are considered to be reasonable demands. One researcher stated that it is easier for a field person to reject certain research requests as not feasible when responding to a researcher — who is not intimately acquainted with operational realities — than to another practitioner who is fully aware of what research functions can be fulfilled within the bounds of the practice role.

In addition, having seen how the data were acquired, having filled out forms that seemed appropriate and useful, having helped in putting data together and interpreting it, those so involved not only become familiar with methods and findings, but also often develop a personal identification with the research and a commitment to move forward with it in the direction in which it leads. It was the view of those interviewed in the study that such involvement in conducting research is conducive to subsequent research utilization.

This general point is confirmed in a study by Rich (1975: 244). He indicates that "decisions concerning how information will be collected influence decisions concerning how information will be used." In order to contribute to more effective utilization of information resources, he recommends that

> policy-makers should be involved in the decisions concerning what information to collect. They should continue to be involved in decisions concerning how the information will be processed and used.

Flanagan (1961) reports that when he compared two applied research projects, greater utilization occurred in the one in which ultimate users took part in collecting data and in assessing the results. In another instance, Chesler and Flanders (1967) tell how a study was turned from a stalemate to a productive venture when the user group was invited to participate in determining procedures.

The social psychological factors related to such participation have been discussed by Schmuck (1968). The building of trust between research and operational people is seen by him as a vital consideration in utilization. Collaborative activity during the course of a study, he indicates, can stimulate such trust. A U.S. Department of Health, Education, and Welfare (1963) examination of the issue reports that attitude change in the direction of commitment to research findings is brought about by the user's sense of participation in creating the results.

UTILIZATION OF RESEARCH IS FACILITATED WHEN RELEVANT OPERATIONAL STAFF PARTICIPATE IN THE FORMULATION OF RECOMMENDATIONS

"The jump between findings and recommendations is diffiuclt," said one respondent. "It involves the oughts — what to do about what you find out." In many instances researchers find this their most troubling area, the one in which they are the least competent to make a contribution. Too often they respond by withdrawing from responsibility for action. This is unfortunate from the standpoint of utilization because operational staff perceive findings without prescriptions to be confusing or barren.

One obvious solution to this dilemma is to engage operational people who are acquainted with the application setting in designing appropriate possible courses of action. A researcher working on a team basis with operational people can interpret the data accurately to those who can apply it and make sure that the applications remain true to what is known, including the limitations of the data.

This type of role-differentiated collaboration takes researchers "off the hook" of making judgments in matters about which they lack appropriate competency, but keeps them "hanging in there" in following through with their data along responsible, efficacious lines. A number of comments in the interviews both describe and espouse such an approach:

> The researcher in our agency has been active in working with involved people in developing policies and applications from the research. He gave information to the staff group, and they collaborated together in making definite recommendations.
>
> Initially, a report was made by the research person. It was tentative and involved a process whereby he teamed up with others. A set of recommendations came out of this; but they reflected the views of the professional staff. Research was only one input. The recommendations had to be stated in such a way as not to step on the toes of certain professionals. Also, a good professional case had to be made for following those recommendations. The staff group later monitored the recommendations to see that people followed through.

These procedures were seen by respondents as supporting positive follow-through with the research in their respective agency settings.

The academic researcher, states Sharpe (1975: 23) is a skeptic by nature. He is

> only too aware of the precarious edifice of knowledge on which he is perched...the prisoner of Beatrice Webb's two-faced intellectual master, "the spirit that affirms and the spirit that denies."

This skepticism partially explains the reluctance of some

social researchers, when situated in an operations research setting, to be willing to act on information. Nonetheless, that situation demands a relaxation of this stance and the adoption of another. Rosenblatt (1968) found that failure of practitioners to use research resulted from the reluctance of researchers to put theories into operational terms that practitioners could understand and test. Likert and Lippitt (1963) suggest a set of guidelines based on their extensive work with practitioners in organizational settings. They feel it essential to aid practitioners in planning and executing steps of action in the specific situation, including creative and realistic thinking around questions such as "What would happen if?" User groups themselves, these authors state, should be encouraged to discover appropriate applications of findings. This process can be aided, they say, by organizing data in such a way that it "presses for action."

UTILIZATION OF RESEARCH IS FACILITATED BY ACTIVE DIFFUSION OF INFORMATION AND RECOMMENDATIONS AMONG OPERATIONAL PEOPLE IN THE AGENCY AND RELEVANT EXTERNAL SYSTEMS

Inscribing recommendations on paper is not a sure route to utilization. Recommendations have to be considered, debated, traded off, and molded into specific courses of action. Respondents indicated several activities that promote the weighing of recommendations within the organization.

Directing Communications at Particular Audiences

Persons within an organization have different concerns. What may be relevant to one group, let us say the operational staff, may not appear to be relevant to another, say, the management group:

You must draw the right people's attention to the right bits.

Reports of recommendations may be written in different lengths, with different slants, or with different language, depending on the audience:

> Reports should have less jargon, be shorter, with different pieces going to different audiences.

A separate short report to management, for example, giving the recommendations derived from the research data, is recommended:

> The report went to social services committee — we added a separate management report, giving concise recommendations.

Moriarty (1967) takes note of the need to get the right material into the right hands at the right time. Elsewhere (Craig, 1975), the point is made in this way:

> Make sure the right people get the right information. A line staff member needs certain detailed feedback about day-to-day performance. A supervisor needs information to compare the effectiveness of different approaches. An agency director is more interested in impact on the objective. The board needs to know about community reactions.

This theme recurred throughout the interviews. It fell into several categories and will be reiterated with a different emphasis in different chapters.

Interpreting Recommendations Assertively

Over and over again respondents pointed out that research findings and recommendations had to be communicated assertively and on a sustained basis within the organization. New understandings and truths set down on paper were no assurance that organizational behavior of any kind would change. Sometimes aggressive advocacy was suggested:

> The researcher has to be able to sell his wares. He has to be a bit of a salesman and even a con man on occasion. He has to point out advantages, economic savings, and practical gains. The group around the research officer put energy behind this and steered it through the organization. We kept people informed and leaned on them when necessary. When certain staff were resistant, we got the support of the director and breathed down their necks.

Others spoke of a more subdued form of research activism:

> We spent a lot of time in the department clarifying and interpreting the material with members of the staff. We circulated reports and made personal contacts. We asked for comments, answered their questions, and allayed their fears. Good telephone contact helped.

In other cases a reactive rather than proactive mode was called for:

> We waited for people to show interest and curiosity. It isn't useful to turn out findings endlessly. You have to look for signs of need or concern and take those opportunities to present materials.

Dissemination can be pleasant:

> We got the information back to people through a symposium format at midday, with wine and cheese served to give the occasion a light touch.

Apparently there is no single formula for advancing research products. The need for a forward-leaning posture is generally agreed upon, however.

Glaser and Taylor (1969) indicate that one of the

distinguishing features of the more successful applied research projects they studied was a high rate of communication, with active project staff efforts to induce interest and cooperation. Unco, Inc. (1973) studied research endeavors in three state departments of welfare and came out with a communication model as best defining instances of successful utilization of technical research. A well-articulated structure for communicating results and implications was found to be vital for effective utilization.

Using Existing Organizational Machinery To Promote Research Results

It was suggested that research results be channeled into appropriate organizational units and events in order to obtain official and concrete review of them:

> Information should be actively considered, not just passed around. It should be tied in with regular agency business, such as placing it on the agenda of the meetings of an appropriate group.
> We discussed the report formally at the management team meeting, and at the assistant director meetings. We set deadlines for pieces of implementation and kept the spotlight on this one.
> We prepared a series of working documents to be reviewed by different administrative groups.

The comments of the respondents have been echoed (Craig, 1975) as follows:

> Use existing channels of communication and decision-making in the agency, both formal and informal.

Providing Interim Feedback on an In-Process Basis

Reports and recommendations are often viewed as

something that materialize at a point where the research activity is nearing termination. A process approach presupposes recurring, two-way interaction and feedback as the research proceeds. The bi-directionality is indicated in the following pair of comments:

> Take people along with you. Give them pieces of information along the way.
> We had a mixed study group involved in planning the project. There were long consultations in which we obtained their ideas as information was fed back to them.

The character of interim feedback and its potential practical utility is evidenced in the following:

> If the research is to be meaningful, the seeds have to be sown early. We have to prepare the groundwork by involving the staff people who will be affected and members of the [city] council social services committee. I make sure members of the committee hear about progress in the research on a continuing basis. I invite their comments and attempt to allay their doubts or suspicions. It is important to keep the issue before committee members so it is not forgotten or sprung on them just at budget time.

This remark indicates the importance of including the governing or sponsoring body of the agency among the various participants in the sociotechnical process. Rich (1975) and Mercer et al. (1964) speak to the utility of "continuous" feedback with potential users during the course of a study.

UTILIZATION OF RESEARCH IS FACILITATED BY DEVELOPMENT ACTIVITIES THAT TRANSLATE RECOMMENDATIONS INTO SPECIFIC PROCEDURES

In several of the departments studied, the research staff followed the research process beyond the point at which recommendations were made and accepted. They took further responsibility for initial operationalization of recommendations in the form of procedures, guidelines, or forms that would be necessary in following through on implications of the research. In all instances this activity was performed jointly with relevant field or management people who were intimately familiar with the context of applications. These groups, called development teams, project teams, or developent panels, engaged in pilot work in order to test the feasibility of recommendations and to acquire an understanding of the practical form they would take. In some instances designated research staff, development officers, were given a specialized role related to this function. To illustrate:

> The research officer worked with the field staff to follow up on the research. It was a piloting effort in which a staff group got together to tease out problems of implementation. As these details were worked out, they issued two additional reports.

In one situation development work of this nature took place without a formal designation of roles. The circumstances suggest some of the contextural factors in development work. The research officer involved was a qualified social worker who had been employed in this same department for a number of years. He knew the professional field staff well, and they were acquainted with him in his previous activity as a practitioner. Because the agency manager restricted research work at the administrative level, the research staff found it necessary to focus much of its effort at practice problems in area field offices.

In addition, the research unit was structurally joined with the training unit under one administrator. Consequently, it became involved in various ways with educational programs for the staff. This research director described a development activity regarding assessment of nursing home arrangements for clients. Following a study that indicated services and facilities were often mismatched with client need, the research officer worked closely with staff within the nursing home settings to develop assessment forms that would allow clients to be placed more beneficially.

One research director felt that development staff need to have special qualifications and talents. They should be, he said, down-to-earth, outgoing, interested in practical aspects of management and practice, comfortable with operational people, and with much drive and enthusiasm that is necessary to keep a staff group motivated through the difficult period of molding new procedures and programs. The stereotypic staid, detached research worker would not, he felt, be equal to this task.

These comments regarding a development stage are particularly significant because *this form of activity is perhaps the least understood and least exhibited of the full set in the process continuum*. Nevertheless, there are writings that support and rationalize this function. A research utilization model that this writer proposed included development as a basic component (Rothman, 1974, 1980). Guba (1968) includes a similar stage, which he describes as directed toward the identification of operating problems and the formulation of solutions to these. This activity is characterized by such terms as "invention," "fabrication," and "testing." Garvey and Griffith (1967) take the position that a research-based innovation should be seen as a trial only, with built-in procedures for modification based on proper evaluation. Unco, Inc. (1973) in their model refer to demonstration that includes: demonstrating relevance to the user's methods of operating; establishing feasibility under those circumstances; and determining whether implementation can meet prior established performance objectives. According to Lippitt and Havelock (1968), a less elaborate form of development can be undertaken, anticipatory in nature, that involves simulation or role playing of implementation. In studying research programs in various applied organizations, Van de Vall et al. (1976: 162) gathered data on a range of research tasks: diagnosing the problem situation, designing policies (recommended actions), and development of problem solutions. It was their conclusion that, when all three aspects were covered in a research program, there was a greater likelihood of implementation than when a fewer number of these aspects were included: "The broader the operational range of applied social research, the higher the degree of utilization for organizational policy."

UTILIZATION OF RESEARCH IS FACILITATED BY CREATING "MIXED" INSTRUMENTALITIES THROUGH WHICH PROCESS ACTIVITIES MAY TAKE PLACE

Participation of key persons in the research process has been underscored. Respondents made many observations and suggestions regarding how they have involved people in the process. Meetings and group activities of various kinds were described. Four different types of instrumentalities became evident: (1) permanent groups, (2) ad hoc groups, (3) research seminars, and (4) new project seminars.

Permanent Representative: Mixed Research-Operations Group

"Research liaison groups" or "mixed groups" made up of persons from various divisions meet on a permanent basis. Persons from the various agency units act as representatives. These groups facilitate the flow of information and provide the mechanism for feedback throughout the organization. The following two respondents state their purpose and structure:

We have a research liaison group that meets bimonthly. I encourage an information-sharing group from various units.

People can demand research and evaluate, suggest, and make criticisms in progress.

Our research liaison group is a linking committee. A member of each unit of the department and the research team meet once a quarter to hash over research activities and needs.

Ad Hoc, Project, or Problem Focused: Mixed Research-Operations Group

This type of group also involves a "flexible balance of research and operational staff." The ad hoc groups may take the form of "project teams," "development teams," or "working parties." They are "mixed, relevant, and task centered." They may be composed of researchers, the director and operational staff, including principal social workers, and seek to "clarify and define the problem and indicate the need for research," and "to try out and evaluate new ideas."

Seminars Outside of the Normal Agency Schedules and Pressures

Seminars for mixed groups can be held outside of usual agency time arrangements (evenings or afternoons, for example, in a peaceful setting, away from the agency site). This creates a "more open and relaxed climate" in which people can examine issues and needs in a careful and unhurried way:

> Researchers are not likely to get recognition from either other agency people or from an academic community. They are isolated. We have set up a monthly researcher-management seminar devoid of immediate task pressures. Researchers have an opportunity to stand out in that type of environment.

New-Project Seminars of Interested Research and Operational Staff

New project seminars are described as change oriented and exploratory. They can be "staffed by the planning department" and, as one researcher indicated, have been "seen as subversive and antimanagement." Another researcher described the new-project seminars as:

> a way of looking at gaps — seeing what is being done and, therefore, what is left to do.

Another researcher labels the seminars a "proactive social action model":

> These seminars serve as a change agent in the department. The new-project seminars search out and set up new procedures, then turn them over to operating units for ongoing administration.

The new-project seminars serve some of the functions of development teams, but they are, apparently, more contemplative and critical in outlook.

Each of the above mechanisms has a different slant. The permanent group provides a continuous structure for carrying out the research-planning process and for legitimating the function. The ad hoc group is oriented toward a specific task or problem and is created as the need arises. Seminars provide a relaxed atmosphere, facilitating creative thinking and supporting the research unit. The new-project seminar acts as a mechanism for pinpointing weaknesses or failures within the organization and also for introducing outside ideas and ways of operating into the organization. Each instrumentality facilitates involvement of relevant persons in the research process; and one or another may be appropriate to a given organizational situation, based on the circumstances, including the stage of development of the research function within the organization.

Various writers have emphasized the need for collaborative interaction between researchers and operational people: Jung and Lippitt (1966), Glaser et al. (1967), and McClelland

(1968). Joly (1967) decries the tendency to rely on individual effort and to underplay interdisciplinary teams of practitioners and researchers. Havelock (1968), indeed, asserts that one of the major tasks of research-oriented change agents is the creation of collaborative temporary systems of researchers and practitioners, building these into more permanent structures when this is called for. The need for complementary differential roles within a pattern of close collaboration is recognized (see, for example, Lundberg, 1966).

UTILIZATION OF RESEARCH IS FACILITATED BY RELATING TIME APPROPRIATELY TO PROCESS FUNCTIONS

There was considerable agreement among those interviewed, particularly researchers, that time pressures were a pervasive problem in these agency settings. One respondent describes the atmosphere:

> The planning process in the agency has a crisis feeling to it. We feel the crush because the director needs lots of information and overloads the research function. We aren't given the time and necessary backing to prepare the research adequately and get it considered in good order.

The view was that the agency demands "quick answers" and that there is a sense among operational staff that research "takes too long." Researchers feel these pressures keenly:

> There are unrealistic time deadlines for research. This has a destructive effect. We lose further credibility this way because it is made to appear that we fail to deliver the goods.

Various suggestions were made concerning how to deal with time considerations.

Allocate Time for Social Process Functions

Accepting the notion that research utilization involves a

sociotechnical process, time has to be allowed to take account of both aspects of the phenomenon. Providing time for the social aspects may mean scaling down usual expectancies concerning research productivity. One research department placed a great deal of emphasis on process, a position strongly supported by both the manager and the research director. A newsletter report describes the work of the research section:

> A certain amount of the section's output is informal and discursive, particularly on the level of how to use and interpret information. While there is much recorded information on which this work is based, the process of guidance and interpretation is less amenable to recording and therefore the total output of the section is inadequately represented by its written outputs — *particularly as reports are not seen as ends in themselves* — [emphasis added].

What is revealed is acceptance that time and energy have to be allocated — and quite rightly so — to the social process dimension in calculating total research effort. Time needs to be structured into the agency operations so that staff at all levels may read, study, discuss, provide feedback into the process, and use the research results:

> Allow time in schedules and plans for the research process. People need to understand why and how to use research. This is not a diversion and peripheral to the main job, but basic time and activity required for full treatment.

Make space and time within the organization to act on information was the message given.

Strategic Timing

Other aspects of time-use were also suggested; for example, timing of research activity so as to move ahead when staff is particularly concerned about a certain problem or issue, or when the community is calling for more information to justify continuing a particular program. In other words, timing in the strategic sense of "striking while the iron is hot," was pointed to as an ingredient of process. Related to this was the concept of building on studies cumulatively. One study can provide the stimulus and rationale for another:

> Research project A can lead or set the stage for research project B and so on. A rolling effect takes place; e.g., home helps led to meals-on-wheels.

Parsimony in Time-Use

Parsimony was another time-related consideration. This suggests buying time by selecting only the most critical studies as perceived by the organization, including a reasonable number of short-term studies, using available data whenever possible, involving operational staff to assist in carrying out research tasks, and so on.

Careful Planning of Research Work

Proper planning in use of time was stressed by several respondents. This is counterpoint to opportunistic responsiveness as it involves a preplanned and structured program. Actually, a viable research process may require both approaches, used in conjunction with one another. Some elements of research planning that were suggested include:

(1) Advance warning is important: We in the research group should get earlier warning of things that are coming in.
(2) Set priorities: Have a set of priorities laid out with management in advance so that research can be planned and well timed. Have priorities for research as well as planning of services.
(3) Anticipate decisions: The research section should be more active in creating a program of research and should be less ad hoc. Anticipate decision areas by being alert and initiate research accordingly.

(4) Do not have research linger on: Set realistic deadlines for reports. Put aside time in the agency to consider them systematically.

(5) Have a broad basic strategy: There is a need to parry the frequent ad hoc requests for information. Work out a year-long program and get it accepted by the Social Services Committee. Section and division staff should give ideas — research staff should discuss and select among these. Set time schedules and priorities. The senior management team must approve. Then the Social Services Committee approves. The ideas come up from the field people, but the research staff should put them together into a comprehensive program.

Another researcher suggested planning a stable research program by building into such a plan slack time for research staff that would be given over to emergent research needs as they arise unexpectedly. In this way both comprehensive/stable and responsive/ad hoc functions would be provided for.

Differences in time perspectives between researchers and operational people have been widely noted in the literature. Donnison (1972: 535), in commenting on policy research, laments that by the time the data are in, "the policy questions will change: so will the parties in power and the structure of the ministries." Abrams (1974) believes it is important for researchers to clarify time dimensions with organizations requesting research before any data-gathering commences. Rosenblatt (1968) found one of the main reasons given by practitioners for not using research findings was lack of time within their practice situation to make the necessary applications. The question of timing is addressed by Davis and Salasin (1975). They propose taking advantage of informal occasions, such as a cocktail party, or formal events, such as the passage of new legislation, to interpret research and promote its use.

AN APPLICATION CHECKLIST FOR PROCESS FACTORS

**Participation of Operational People in
Defining Research Problems**

☐ Has a range of agency interests and roles been involved in defining research problems (managers, line staff, middle-level managers and supervisors, members of the governing board, community people)?

☐ Has the research staff actively "listened" in order to discern issues and needs?

☐ Has the research staff probed and otherwise assisted in order to bring out concerns and sharpen issues?

**Participation of Operational People
in Carrying Out Research**

☐ Have operational people been engaged in planning for data-gathering?

☐ Have they been involved in gathering the data?

☐ Have they been engaged in encouraging others to provide information?

☐ Have they been brought into interpreting the data?

**Participation of Operational People
in Formulating Recommendations**

☐ Have agency staff been asked to review findings in order to derive action implications?

☐ Have researchers assisted in this by holding applications within reasonable bounds of the data while stimulating creative thinking about viable action implications?

**Dissemination of Information
and Recommendations to Relevant parties**

☐ Have different audiences been targets for different types of information?

☐ Has assertive information giving and interpretation been carried out?

☐ Has opportunity been provided for exchange about the meaning and application of findings?

☐ Have existing committees, newsletters, and other organizational machinery been used to disseminate information?

☐ Has there been feedback to relevant audiences during the course of the process rather than only at the end?

Provision for Development Activities

☐ Have relevant operational people who are familiar with key application areas been brought together to explore implementation steps and procedures?

☐ Have specific development instrumentalities been established, such as researcher/practitioner task groups, development teams, and so on?

☐ Have piloting activities been considered?

☐ Have procedural guides, such as handbooks, been produced as a result of these activities?

Time Considerations

☐ Has time been set aside within the organization specifically to allow for social and technical process activities?

☐ Has there been a sense of strategic movement in taking advantage of organizational events — a high level of interest, needs having been dramatized, and the like?

☐ Have priorities been clarified and agreed upon?

☐ Has the principle of parsimony been employed to buy time — drawing upon available data, setting up short-term projects?

☐ Is there provision for early warning of research needs?

☐ Have realistic time lines been established?

REFERENCES

ABRAMS, MARK (1974) "Social surveys, social theory and social policy." SSRC Newsletter 24 July: 11-14.

CHESLER, MARK and M. FLANDERS (1967) "Resistance to research and research utilization: the death and life of a feedback attempt." Journal of Applied Behavioral Science 3: 467-487.

CRAIG, DOROTHY (1975) "A hip pocket guide to planning and evaluation." Mental Health Skills Lab, School of Social Work, University of Michigan, Ann Arbor.

DAVIS, HOWARD and SUSAN SALASIN (1975) "The utilization of evaluation," pp. 621-666 in Elmer Struening and Marcia Guttentag (eds.) Handbook of Evaluation Research, Vol. 1. Beverly Hills, CA: Sage.

DONNISON, DAVID (1972) "Research for policy". Minerva 10, 4: 519-536.

ENGSTROM, G. A. (1970) "Research utilization: the challenge of applying SRS research." Welfare in Review 2: 1-7.

FLANAGAN, JOHN C. (1961) "Case studies on the utilization of behavioral science research," pp. 36-46 in Case Studies in Bringing Behavioral Science into Use. Studies in the Utilization of Behavioral Science, Vol. 1. Palo Alto, CA: Institute for Communication Research, Stanford University.

GARVEY, W. D. and B. C. GRIFFITH (1967) "Communication in a science: the system and its modification," pp. 16-36 in A. de Reuck and J. Knight (eds.) Communication in Science: Documentation and Automation. A Ciba Foundation Boston: Little, Brown.

GLASER, EDWARD M., H. S. COFFEE, J. B. MARKS, and I. B. SARASON (1967) Utilization of Applicable Research and Demonstration Results. Los Angeles: Human Interaction Research Institute.

GLASER, EDWARD M. and S. TAYLOR (1969) Factors Influencing the Success of Applied Research. Washington, DC: National Institute of Mental Health, Department of Health, Education, and Welfare.

GUBA, Egon G. (1968) "Development, diffusion and evaluation," pp. 37-63 in T. L. Eidell and J. M. Kitchel (eds.) Knowledge Production and Utilization in Educational Administration. Eugene: Center for the Advanced Study of Educational Administration, University of Oregon.

HAVELOCK, RONALD G. (1968) "New developments in translating theory and research into practice." Presented at the 96th Annual Meeting of the American Public Health Association, Detroit, November.

——— and DAVID A. LINGWOOD (1973) R & D Utilization Strategies and Functions: An Analytical Comparison of Four Systems. Ann Arbor: MI: Institute for Social Research, University of Michigan.

JOLY, JEAN-MARIE (1967) "Research and innovation: two solitudes?" Canadian Education and Research Digest 2: 184-194.

JUNG, CARL and RONALD LIPPITT (1966) "The study of change as a concept in research utilization." Theory Into Practice 2, 1: 25-29.

LIKERT, RENSIS and RONALD LIPPITT (1963) "The utilization of social scinece," in L. Festinger and D. Katz (eds.) Research Methods in the Behavioral Sciences. New York: Dryden.

LIPPITT, RONALD and RONALD HAVELOCK (1968) "Needed research on research utilization," in Research Implication for Educational Diffusion. East Lansing: Department of Education, Michigan State University.

LUNDBERG, CRAIG C. (1966) "Middlemen in science utilization: some notes toward clarifying conversion roles." American Behavioral Scientist 9 (February): 11-14.

MACKIE, R. R. and P. R. CHRISTENSEN (1967) Translation and Application of Psychological Research. Technical Report 716-1. Goleta, CA: Santa Barbara Research Park, Human Factors Research.

McCLELLAND, W. A. (1968) "The process of effecting change." Presidential Address to the Division of Military Psychology, American Psychological Association.

MERCER, J. R., H. F. DINGMAN, and G. TARJAN (1964) "Involvement, feedback, and mutuality: principles for conducting mental health research in the community." American Journal of Psychiatry 121, 3: 228-237.

MORIARTY, EDWARD J. (1967) "Summary of small group recommendations," pp. 72-73 in Communication, Dissemination, and Utilization of Rehabilitation Research Information. Studies in Rehabilitation Counselor Training No. 5 Washington, DC: Joint Liaison Committee of the Council of State Administrators of Vocational Rehabilitation and Rehabilitation Counselor Educators, Department of Health, Education, and Welfare.

RICH, ROBERT F. (1975) "Selective utilization of social science related information by federal policy-makers." Inquiry 13, 3: 239-245.

ROSENBLATT, AARON (1968) "The practitioners use and evaluation of research." Social Work 13: 53-59.

ROTHMAN, JACK (1980) Social R & D: Research and Development in the Human Services. Englewood Cliffs, NJ: Prentice-Hall.

——— (1974) Planning and Organizing for Social Change: Action Principles from Social Science Research. New York: Columbia University Press.

SCHMUCK, RICHARD (1968) "Social psychological factors in knowledge utilization," pp. 143-173 in T. L. Eidell and J. M. Kitchel (eds.) Knowledge Production and Utilization in Educational Administration. Eugene: Center for the Advanced Study of Educational Administration, University of Oregon.

SHARPE, L. J. (1975) "The social scientist and policy-making: some cautionary thoughts and transatlantic reflections." Journal of Policy and Politics 4, 2: 7-34.

SMITH, GILBERT (1972) "Research policy: 'pure' and 'applied.'" British Hospital Journal and Social Science Review (April): 723-724.

TWAIN, DAVID, ELEANOR HARLOW, and DONALD MERWIN (1974) Research and Human Services: A Guide to Collaboration for Program Development. Washington, DC: National Institute of Mental Health, Department of Health, Education, and Welfare.

UNCO, INC. (1973) Communication Model for the Utilization of Technical Research (CMUTR) Study: Utilization of Advanced Management Innovations Within State Departments of Public Welfare. Washington, DC: Unco, Inc.

U.S. Department of Health, Education, and Welfare (1963) Research Utilization in Aging: An Exploration. Washington, DC: Government Printing Office.

VAN de VALL, MARK, CHERYL BOLAS and TAI S. KANG (1976) "Applied social research in industrial organizations: an evaluation of functions, theory, and methods." Journal of Applied Behavioral Science 12, 2: 158-177.

Chapter 4

ORGANIZATIONAL CLIMATE:
Attitudes and Relationships

The social psychological climate of attitude and relationship within an organization appears to be yet another influence on research utilization. Respondents in our study recurrently mentioned attitudes and interaction among researchers and operational people as factors that made a difference in use of research. Comments along these lines were made more frequently, perhaps, than any others. Interpersonal linkage and the attitudes that promote such linkage clearly merit attention.

Other investigators have also pointed out the significance of this dimension. Pelz and Andrews (1976), for example, studied diverse applied research organizations performing R & D functions. They found that facets of organizational climate, such as communication and motivation, were critical to effecting productivity. Two recent studies dealing specifically with research utilization are of particular interest. Caplan (1977: 194-195) has presented statisticial evidence to show that the "two communities" theory best accounts for distance between researchers and policy makers (as compared with theories that place blame on inappropriate behavior by researchers or the constraints under which operational people work). In his view:

> Theories of underutilization with the greatest degree of explanatory power are those emphasizing the existence of a gap between social scientists and policy makers due to differences in values, language, reward systems, and social and personal affiliations.... Social scientists would be well advised to pay close attention to...lack of interaction among social scientists and policy makers as a major reason for nonuse.

Caplan indicates that the phenomenon he is describing is made up of an interaction dimension and a dimension he called "perspectives" — attitudes, values, and ideology. Increased interaction without changes in perspectives, according to Caplan, will accomplish little.

The other pertinent study was conducted by Patton and his associates (1977: 155) and comprised a follow-up of 170 evaluations performed by HEW in the early 1970s. Political feasibility considerations, as the researchers had expected, played an important part in whether evaluations were acted upon. But another set of considerations, not anticipated by the investigators, was found to be of comparable moment. They refer to this as "personal factors" and indicate that it is composed of such things as interest, enthusiasm, commitment, determination, and caring. According to the authors, this factor

> consistently arose in the comments of decisionmakers, evaluators, and project officers — a factor so crucial that respondents repeatedly pointed to it as the single most important element in the utilization process.... When the personal factor emerges, evaluations have an impact; when it is absent, there is a marked absence of impact.

We are not able to say whether social-psychological factors were more significant than structural or process factors in the organizations we studied. We can only report that they were seen as notable by our informants along with the others. More importantly, we can delineate relevant components of attitude and interaction, and indicate ways in which these components can serve specifically to facilitate utilization.

As mentioned, respondents addressed these social-psychological factors with considerable frequency. Many of their comments centered on deficiencies in attitudes or relationships on the part of the researchers and operational people. These "criticisms" were so widely and animatedly expressed that a proper detailing of them seems necessary in order to understand the context of facilitative attitudes and relationships that were also identified. The format of this chapter will vary somewhat from the others in that we will start with what amounts to an analysis of perceived deficiencies in communication. Perceived deficits of operational people will be indicated, followed by perceived deficits of researchers. The positive side then will be presented, including concrete attitudes and modes of relating that counteract these impediments.

The presentation will also vary in another way. Because of the volume of information concerning social-psychological variables and the space limitations for this discussion, the critique will be based almost entirely on the interviews with few references to related material from the literature.

In initiating this discussion, it is well to recognize that we are dealing with different perspectives and values, not with established standards of right and wrong. For example, researchers who were interviewed frequently chided operational people for what were declared to be incorrect uses of research. Information is frequently taken out of context; it is used prematurely; it is construed as a weapon rather than a statement of truth; and it serves the purposes of strategy rather than enlightenment. A typical comment was that "management wants to leave out certain information that doesn't suit its purposes, leading to a lack of balance in the report."

This issue is not a simple one. Two conversations a few

hours apart with the research person and the director of a particular agency highlight the dilemma. The researcher was dismayed that the director had used data from a certain study in a planning decision prior to the time that the data had been adequately validated. The sample was small, not sufficiently representative, and the measuring instruments were not fully developed. The researcher did not have confidence that the findings were strong enough to guide specific action. The agency director brought up the same situation in his interview. His complaint was that the researcher was too academic and antiseptic in her approach. In his view he was operating in a complex environment in which there were a great many uncertainties. In most cases he was forced to take action with little or no information. In the instance in question he had available a modicum of data, gathered in his particular operational situation to inform a decision that had to be taken at the time. He claimed that this offered a greater opportunity to act on the basis of information than normally is his fortune; to fail to do so would have been irresponsible. In his view the researcher was not sufficiently attuned to the realities of agency operations or to the circumstances surrounding an agency administrator's use of information.

It is difficult to declare who is fundamentally correct or in error in this dispute. The two sides reflect the kinds of cross-pressures that exist in operations research. These are natural tensions that appropriately should be at play continually and that need to be resolved interactively in particular circumstances by the dual set of interests. Without resolution we are left with the uncomfortable feeling that research of any kind, like Kettering's view of logic, emerges as merely an organized way of going wrong with confidence.

Deficits of Operational People

Both researchers and directors cited in profusion defective

attitudes and modes of operation by agency staff (including directors) that they found to stand in the way of productive use of research. Directors were no more restrained than researchers in expressing such criticisms. Many of the directors were either professionally committed to the idea of research, or administratively bound to the cost-efficient use of research that was taking place in their agency situation. Caplan, too, found that the policy makers he interviewed had surprisingly positive attitudes toward research. For them, it was a source of frustration and irritation that some program and field staff were taking an uncooperative stance with regard to this available agency resource. These observations concerning operating staff attitudes and ways of work fell into various categories.

Force of Custom

It was said that a certain inertia and unthinking conservatism exists in agency situations. As one director put it: "Things get repeated based on custom. The system runs itself, but it doesn't criticize itself." Staff were described as "an undisciplined group that just wants to get on with the job." And senior people were found, often, to be "set in their ways." This leads to "chronic resistance to change" or "inherent resistance." Consequently, "it is difficult to convince people that their attitudes should bend to research facts."

Attachment to Particular Services

Sometimes it is not generalized inertia that inhibits change, but rather an emotional involvement with particular existing forms of service. This implicates not only the staff, but also the sponsoring or governing body of the agency. It was stated, for example, that there are "appealing" and "unappealing" client groups. On the appealing side, those mentioned included children, the handicapped, and the aged. Among the unappealing were multiproblem families, juvenile delin-

quents, and battered wives. It appeared to be a matter of one
clientele who could be blamed for their difficulties and
another who were not to be blamed. For example, battered
wives were viewed by some as grown adults who acted volun-
tarily in entering into a marriage: "They should have known
better," or "they made their choice and now they should live
with it." These sentiments were said to reflect community attitudes that sometimes influenced or constrained the staff.

Defensiveness Against Criticism

One of the major blocks to serious attention to research, it
was said, is the tendency of operational people to feel
threatened by information that implies a criticism of their
practices. This applies to executives and to field staff:

> The administration has responded nervously to forthright
> recommendations for change when there is an inferred
> criticism of their work.
> People in operational positions are suspicious of research and
> feel threatened that their practices will be called into question.
> Evaluation can be painful.

The sensitivity to criticism may stem, in part, from the
underdeveloped state of knowledge and technology in the
human services. Professionals lack basic confidence in what
they are doing and shrink from having this insecurity "rubb-
ed in their eyes."

Loss of Autonomy

The sense of threat that is felt is not exclusively based on
tender feelings. There is also a premonition of "consequences," including constriction of one's independence of
action. This was expressed in several different ways:

> Staff members are jealous of their autonomy. Research is
> sometimes viewed as an infringement on their professional
> judgment. Some managers see research as a threat to their

control over agency affairs.

Social workers are resistant to having their work analyzed. They are defensive about someone from the outside telling them what to do.

Loss of Status or Role

Research is sometimes experienced as an intrusion on organizational patterns and arrangements. One's position in the hierarchy might be changed undesirably — prestige might be diminished; departmental relationships might be jostled:

> The old boss objected to the loss of his empire. And his staff did not want to be transferred to a new and uncertain situation.
>
> Each departmental group thinks its empire is the most important. They ward off research that upsets their position.

Climate of Pressure

The environmental context in which operational personnel function was characterized as harried and overpressured. Demands to examine research and apply it to work tasks was seen as still an additional burden. These time pressures and multiple job requirements were viewed by our informants as realistic rather than contrived. The objective work situation may lead to a subjective outlook that is hostile to research:

> There are many pressures to ameliorate immediate problems. Staff are overloaded and anxious. There is lack of time to go into matters in depth, such as studying research reports.
>
> The field staff is frustrated and fatigued. They have a natural limited endurance. There isn't a wide consensus that taking time to deal with research will bring relief.

It was pointed out that the time pressures also interfere with staff willingness to take part in the data-gathering, filling out forms, and other aspects of the conduct of research.

Intuitive Intellectual Style

An obstacle to research utilization is a cognitive outlook by certain operational people that places a high value on "working things through" on a case-by-case basis. There is a reliance on personal judgment, past experience, and a "feeling for the situation":

> There is a conceptual problem on the part of some people. Managers sometimes act on the basis of hunch and intuition, and it is difficult to break this pattern. Pressures of time and unpredictable political circumstances intensify the conceptual problem.

Misunderstanding of Research

Operational staff were said to have insufficient background in research, with the result that they do not know how to participate in, and take advantage of, the research process. This takes several forms:

> Some staff don't see the significance of research. It is a novel idea that they are suspicious of. They lack adequate preparation and understanding. Some managers aren't comfortable with figures and can't interpret basic statistics.
>
> There is an attitude among operational people that "we do the real work." If you are not involved in providing services, you are viewed as extra baggage. Researchers are viewed in that way.
>
> People can't state a problem adequately. They ask for information on overly broad and vague questions.
>
> There are unrealistic time deadlines for research. These outlandish time expectations have a destructive effect. Researchers fail to deliver the goods and lose credibility even more. People want fast answers, and there is pressure on the research staff to react too quickly.

Anti-Intellectual Radicalism

A smaller number of comments pertained to a radical perspective that was inimical to research. Research was viewed as a tool for containing situations that cry out for massive action rather than deliberative reflection:

Some members of the staff exhibit an obscurantist attitude — a false radicalism that says, "Let's get more of everything, regardless of economic considerations." They feel that an emotional campaign will get more for the poor and disadvantaged than any amount of research. In their view, research plays into the hands of those who want to go slowly and give little.

These characterizations of operational people do not represent a global, all-encompassing portrait. While some informants took a wide sweep in their criticisms, others made their critique conditional and particularized, implicating only a minority of "bad actors." Others to whom we spoke went out of their way to laud the general performance of operational people within their organizations. A research director put it this way:

> There is plenty of intellectual ability and self-reliance among a wide range of staff members. They are people with good ideas who are doing important work, but large organizations, such as this one, also place restrictive limits on staff and really underestimate them. It is up to the research staff to encourage them and to bring forth their contributions.

What is reality and what is perception? How deep do these criticisms cut, and what proportion of operational staff are implicated? These are questions that cannot be answered here but require further documentation.

Deficits of Researchers

Just as directors joined in the criticism of operational people, researchers found much fault with the attitudinal and behavioral presentation of their fellow researchers. Negative evaluations of researchers, however, were more focused; they concentrated on a pattern of aloofness or detachment researchers were said to exhibit. The aloofness pattern had several manifestations.

"Ivory Tower" Arrogance

It was felt by many of those who were interviewed that researchers keep themselves distanced from operational people. This separateness was described in psychological, social, and programmatic terms. In part it may be accounted for by training that emphasizes objectivity and impartiality in the conduct of one's work. Involvement might result in contamination. Another aspect of this, however, alluded to by some informants, is a demeanor of arrogance or superiority. Being apart from the workaday travail of agency activity is also sometimes combined with being above it. A critical stance becomes merged with a cynical, disdainful one:

> Researchers are seen by our staff as being too academic, too sophisticated, and too remote. They live in an ivory tower and won't come down to learn anything about social work.

Aloofness from Agency Goals

Some researchers, apparently, fail to address themselves to the basic objectives of the agency and to the social problems it is mandated to ameliorate. Their concerns remain overly theoretical in the eyes of operational people:

> Researchers may go off in interests of their own which are not relevant to the key concerns of this organization. Some staff members view them as parasitic because they do not contribute to helping with the real and important problems of the agency.
> Sometimes they get absorbed in technical concerns rather than the here-and-now problems that we are grappling with.

Aloofness from Organizational Involvements

The above criticism covers not only the external goals of the agency, but also its internal difficulties and operational patterns. It touches on such considerations as loyalty, identification, and paying one's dues:

Researchers keep themselves away from the "hot seat."
Some staff members think the research section personnel are too protected from the pressures and demands the rest of us face. They don't want to get their hands dirty, and then they come around asking people to fill out more bloody forms.

Aloofness from Contact with Operational Personnel

A more direct form of aloofness is avoidance of personal contact and association with field staff and administration. This low rate of personal contact embraces both informal social relationships "around the office" (chitchat, having lunch together, and so on) and personal association in matters specifically connected with the research endeavor. The "two cultures" phenomenon apparently effects relationships even in areas of specific task relevance:

Research is too much a headquarters-located operation. The research staff is too removed from practitioners. They sometimes seem like strangers in the organization.

Aloofness from Work Demands on Operational People

Here our respondents spoke of lack of awareness of the task environment of operational people and insensitivity to the requirements and demands under which they work. Not being familiar with the realities of operations, it was said, causes researchers to misjudge feasibility about the conduct and application of research:

Research is becoming debased by insensitivity of researchers. They shouldn't ask very busy people to fill out fat forms unnecessarily.

Researchers don't realize the pressures people are under to get the job done, and so there is resentment. You shouldn't impose on people's time and energy without a clear operational objective.

Several of the respondents indicated that aloofness generates lack of trust by operational staff. This in turn has ubiquitous consequences for the way research is received and used.

FACILITATIVE FACTORS

Fortunately, this set of criticisms of operational staff and of researchers was balanced by many favorable observations. In the next sections we will present a series of social-psychological attributes of both sets of actors that were assumed to facilitate research utilization. The facilitative factors were based on two types of comments by our informants: (1) observations about presentation of self that had aided concrete research utilization efforts within the organization, and (2) observations and suggestions concerning what type of presentation or change of presentation would have been more helpful in the situation. During the course of the interviews both types of comments flowed freely and intermingled with one another. It was difficult to sort them out and keep them separated. These facilitative factors, therefore, should be taken as views of "front line" researchers and administrators with a commitment to research utilization about attitudinal and interactional factors that can have a positive impact on use of research. The views are presented in composite fashion from observations about "what worked" and speculations about "what would have worked."

It is interesting to observe that, while most of the critical comments — and the greater variety — were directed at operational staff, the weight of comment about corrective actions was aimed at the research staff. While both operational staff and research staff had been faulted, there was a clear implication that the major momentum for remedy was with the researcher. Analysis of responses revealed a strong emphasis on the skillful *use of communication* in dealing with the social-psychological forces at play. Successful use of research was associated with a vigorous style of communication on the part of researchers, which includes the *active receiving* and *active giving* of communication. We will discuss these in turn. Following the treatment of researchers, we will turn our attention to operational personnel.

UTILIZATION OF RESEARCH IS FACILITATED WHEN RESEARCHERS ENGAGE IN ACTIVE "LISTENING"

Facilitating Behavior by Researchers

There was a widely shared opinion that it is helpful for researchers to "listen" to what is going on in the organization. This listening behavior was characterized as active rather than passive in quality:

> We researchers should try to be more aware of the obligations of the department rather than to carry out our own interests. . . . Also, here we have tried to be the ears of the manager in the department so that we can keep him informed about what needs to be done.
> Researchers should "listen" and take prompts from managers. They must recognize the problems of the manager and not put grit in his way.

In the former instance, the senior research person was given a research and development title. His job description specifically excluded him from daily operational functions, either in research production or service provision, so that he could take in what was going on. The role called for extensive liaison with a wide range of agency members and the recommending of policy. Time was set aside for "being on the scene," "keeping an eye on problems," and "understanding the situation" so that this intelligence could be conveyed to the chief executive officer and molded into research projects. Both researchers speak in terms of what *should* be done; but *should* in these and many other instances actually meant, "these are things we have been doing with good effects; we should keep on doing them — or even increase our activity.

Other researchers should also do these things to have the same effects."

Several respondents indicated the importance of posing concise questions during the listening process in order to clarify and sharpen the issues at hand.

The need to perceive and hear across the camp of researcher and the camp of operator is brought out by Rose (1977: 28), who describes "two different intellectual disciplines, based on contrasting organizations that socialize and reward different kinds of achievements." Davis and Salasin (1975: 651-652) indicate that communication is improved if the researcher "identifies himself with his audience," and these authors recommend "scanning the state of affairs" by paying attention to "informal clues" such as complaints, rumors, signs of low morale, and backstage maneuvering.

UTILIZATION OF RESEARCH IS FACILITATED WHEN RESEARCHERS EMPLOY A STYLE THAT IS RESPONSIVE, RESPECTFUL, AND NONTHREATENING

Respondents indicated that the manner of gauging the organization may be as important as the act itself. These comments appeared to be in juxtaposition to the previously noted bearing of arrogance exhibited by some researchers. Typically:

> We have not imposed information on people. We use a strategy of waiting to be asked and have proved our credibility in this way.
> Researchers shouldn't just barge in and think they know it all. They should be flexible and courteous. They should ask other people to give their opinions about the problem.
> As manager, I have observed that our research staff make themselves acceptable and welcome. They ask, "Can we come to your meeting?" "Would it be convenient?" They act in an agreeable and nonthreatening way, and they take care to explain the purpose of what they are doing.

This approach is an antidote to the demeanor of some researchers that had been described by our respondents as coldly condescending. What is called for is a recognition, as Wilson (1961) points out, that this process is taking place in a web of human relations. Social researchers would do well to apply their ample knowledge of human behavior to their own concrete reality situation. Eash (1968) has observed that the interaction between educational researchers and teachers is often one in which there is an implication that the teacher is inadequate, causing heightened tension and disaffection. Bright (1964) advises researchers to minimize the threat factor in their relationships as resistance is expressed in proportion to the threat that people feel.

UTILIZATION OF RESEARCH IS FACILITATED WHEN RESEARCHERS HAVE AN INTEREST IN OPERATIONAL MATTERS

It was pointed out repeatedly that researchers should express interest in, and appreciation of, the responsibilities of both managers and practitioners. Such appreciation, it was said, serves to strengthen relationships and assure that research undertaken will reflect the needs of, and circumstances faced by, operational people:

> Research people in this field should have very strong applied interests.
> Researchers must be knowledgeable at a very specific operational level.

In several cases it was pointed out that the researcher had a background in the operational field (planning, social work practice), and this greatly facilitated making connections between researchers and field staff. On the other hand, several respondents pointed out that lack of planning interests and experiences had hindered the effectiveness of members of the research staff. Thus, recruiting people with mixed research/operations backgrounds seems desirable. Alternatively, it seems useful to recruit researchers with pronounced applied interests.

These comments are supported by others who have studied the problem. In discussing the role of the behavioral scientist in the medical field, Beckhard (1974) indicates advantages of leaning toward personal investment in health care systems in contrast to the usual stance of professional distance. Van den Ban (1963) states that, unless the researcher has a real interest in the operational problems of the practitioner, utilization will be hindered. Donnison (1972: 532) stresses the importance of this attitudinal set in this way:

> The research workers to look for should, of course, be the most creative and intelligent we can find. But their motivation is equally important and harder to assess. They must have a policy-oriented cast of mind, or be likely to acquire that in time.

UTILIZATION OF RESEARCH IS FACILITATED WHEN RESEARCHERS HAVE AN INTEREST IN ORGANIZATIONAL PROCESSES, INCLUDING ORGANIZATIONAL POLITICS

Familiarity with professional operations without awareness of the impact of the contextual organizational system leads to incomplete understanding and hampers effectiveness. It also sets researchers apart from the life of the organization and the struggles of its members:

> You need competent, practical researchers who have their feet on the ground and understand organizational problems and policies. They need to know how people tick and how change comes about. They must be aware of the political dimension — research as part of the change process. There will be clashes between different factions and interests regarding

organizational matters — it is not a totally objective, rational situation. They must understand this in order not to arrive at naive, unworkable recommendations that have no possibility of being implemented.

Elsewhere, Kogan (1963) found that social work researchers tend to overlook the organizational environment to the detriment of utilization of their products. Churchman (1964: 36) makes the same observation of those in the business field:

> The researcher is apt to find that his recommendations are viewed from the point of view of their effect on a coalition, and not from the point of view of the whole organization. Since the researcher usually doesn't know who belongs to what coalition, and is far from understanding what holds the coalition together...he finds himself in a confusing welter of contradictory reactions.

There are, of course, traps in gaining political awareness and the calculated responses it calls forth. For example, one researcher indicated that there is danger in being seen as a special pleader for particular specializations or interests within the department. He suggested that researchers convey "an overview across the divisions of the organization." What this apparently adds up to is a prescription to be politically informed and at the same time politically skillful.

Another aspect was brought out in numerous interviews. The research staff needs to be close to the chief executive, who, after all, has the power and the resources to make research significant in the organization. Many of the administrators spoke of the research section functioning legitimately as a direct tool of mangement and planning. It was also stated, however, that too much identification with management can fence researchers off from the service staff. Especially in situations where management and line workers are in conflict, the researcher is obliged to tread delicately. Ultimate solutions for these organizational dilemmas were not forthcoming; at the same time there was a clear message that an attempt to avoid them is not compatible with optimizing the research function.

We began this section by stating that listening is not defined as a passive act. Neither is it a totally self-effacing one. Researchers need to be attentive to organizational concerns while maintaining their own intellectual integrity. Listening involves, also, weighing and evaluating and making judgments. As one researcher observed:

> Researchers have to find the right balance between responsiveness or accountability to the organization and freedom for themselves to demonstrate their skills and creativity.

This balance also concerns a dichotomy between being the receiver or the initiator of communication. It is to the latter that we now turn.

UTILIZATION OF RESEARCH IS FACILITATED WHEN ATTITUDES OF RESEARCHERS ENCOURAGE COMMUNICATION WITH OPERATIONAL PEOPLE

This is the analogue to active listening. It is captured in a statement by an informant that the use of research in his agency was aided because researchers "showed a willingness to communicate." This attitude of willingness must, of course, be accompanied by correlative behavior: energy must be applied. Functionally, it turns out that the researcher has the most at stake in this issue. True, operational people may be big losers when the consequences of their professional practices are less than they might be because research was neglected. They do not, however, recognize and feel that loss. It is the researcher who feels unappreciated, frustrated, and diminished when his products are relegated to the organizational junkyard. It behooves the researcher to take the initiative in reaching out (both out of concern for one's sense of personal integrity and because of a responsibility to see that one's efforts serve meaningful professional and social purposes). The essence of this general position was stated in the following:

> Researchers should make an effort to send materials around. They should establish contact with people and make their presence felt. An assertive attitude is necessary.

Rogers (1967; and Shoemaker, 1971) places communication at the heart of the adoption of innovations. His prolific research and writings have consistently stressed the importance of positive communication in furthering the utilization of scientific knowledge. The linkage concepts of Havelock (1969), central to his theory of knowledge utilization, overlap to a considerable degree with the notion of communication. A large number of other social scientists, influenced by these leading figures, have further underlined the significance of communication.

UTILIZATION OF RESEARCH IS FACILITATED WHEN RESEARCHERS PARTICIPATE IN AGENCY MEETINGS WITH OPERATIONAL PEOPLE

The previous discussion emphasized one-on-one interaction. Group activities and committee meetings of various kinds within the agency offer another vehicle for association. Association through meetings gives certain advantages: reaching a moderately large number of people in each contact (but still at the personal level), exploiting established channels of communication, and tying contacts into basic organizational concerns. Such more formalized means of contact should not be the only method relied upon; but, in supplementation to informal personal communication, they can be useful. An observation from an informant states the matter well:

Researchers should get to meetings within the various divisions. We have to make an effort to know when they take place and get ourselves invited. It helps to get yourself placed on the agenda if you want to make sure about being there.

Attendance at meetings covered two categories: basic organizational meetings that deal with regular agency business, and specialized meetings and committees that are concerned with research matters. The first type includes staff meetings and planning sessions that take place continually throughout an organization. The second type includes research seminars, research liaison committees, implementation working parties, study groups, and development teams.

UTILIZATION OF RESEARCH IS FACILITATED WHEN RESEARCHERS MAKE INTERPERSONAL CONTACT IN OPERATIONAL SITUATIONS

One form of assertive communication is direct interpersonal interaction. It was strongly felt by the informants that such person-to-person association either had been beneficial or would have improved matters. These associations can be specifically task oriented or more diffuse in nature. They can be formal or informal. The point was approached from various angles:

> Our research staff isn't office based. They make forays out into the divisions on some pretense or other. They don't come over in an aggressive and high-powered way, but try to be friendly. As a result, they are beginning to get more calls from practitioners for information, or people drop in to see them when visiting headquarters.
>
> The research section involves itself in the activities of the operational branches. It is important to keep alert to situations where you might be needed. Don't be desk bound. Good telephone contact is also very useful.

The research group should get out among the field staff. We sit with people, listen to what they have to say, show them we are there to help.

It has been estimated by Swanson (1966) that a large amount of scientific information is exchanged verbally and informally through face-to-face communication prior to using bibliographic tools. In other words, even among academic scientists informal contact is heavily relied upon. Parker and Paisley (1966) provide evidence that people in applied fields were more dependent upon informal networks than were those in "pure" science areas. In their classic study of diffusion of medical innovations, Coleman et al. (1966) discovered the crucial role of "social intermediaries" (colleagues, detail men) in comparison with impersonal media in influcing physicians to use new drugs. Glaser's (1973) work is consistent, particularly his conclusion that in many situations the "greatest *single* means that can be used to increase information utilization may be personal interaction."

The benefits of various types of group meetings to foster utilization of research have been demonstrated by such researchers as Poser et al. (1964), Crane (1970), Cooper and Archambault (1968), and Van den Ban (1963). Poser and his associates describe a case study in a hospital setting in which meetings between researchers and ward personnel were essential for permitting a workable research environment. Cooper and Archambault illustrate the utility of a conference approach in the vocational rehabilitation field.

UTILIZATION OF RESEARCH IS FACILITATED WHEN RESEARCHERS USE A STYLE OF COMMUNICATION THAT IS INTERPRETIVE AND SUPPORTIVE

Active communication does not imply performance that is brusk, dogmatic, and overbearing. Indeed, many of those we spoke with felt that favorable relationships and positive utilization came about when researchers extended themselves in a way that was supportive, educational, and caring. One person expressed this concisely: "Since practitioners are not oriented to research, help them see the utility of research."

This notion of interpreting and supporting was emphasized in a number of interviews. For example, with respect to interpreting aspects of research:

> There is a lack of awareness by practitioners and managers of how research can be used. I needed to show them only one good example to clear the way.
> Practitioners are not used to dealing with research. You have to give them time and a chance to practice if you want them to develop the skills.
> Explain and clarify things, such as why new forms are being circulated and how they will be used — even if this takes up your time.

The supportive aspect came out in these examples:

> When research supports the going practices in the organization, communicate this. It is encouraging news for the staff. Evaluation that is critical should be communicated in a caring way.

In the study by Poser and his associates (1964) the authors describe the degree of protracted interpretation to clinicians that was necessary in order to further research purposes. Only when the researchers expressed their recognition of the success of the practice already employed by the clinical group was the level of conflict reduced. Davis and Salasin (1975: 647) provide a rationale for supportive interpretation:

> It is important to avoid implications of criticism. If those involved in the change process perceive it as criticism of what they have been doing, they will become resentful and defensive.... . Developing a full understanding of the change is

almost always a good idea. This includes why the change is needed, what is to be changed, now, by whom, when, what benefits can be expected, and what other outcomes can be anticipated. When there is a vacuum created by lack of understanding, it is filled by conjecture.

UTILIZATION OF RESEARCH IS FACILITATED WHEN RESEARCHERS ARE VIGOROUS IN PROMOTING RESEARCH FINDINGS AND RECOMMENDATIONS

This statement is ostensibly at variance with the previous one. It emphasizes the energetic salesperson rather than the patient teacher. Our informants told us that both types of behavior stimulate research utilization. Apparently, researchers should be prepared to perform differentially in both of these ways, depending on circumstances (the organizational setting, the stage in the development of a project, the researcher's personality, the wishes and expectations of operational staff, the kind of relationship that has been established between researchers and operators, and so on).

The view is that momentum is needed to move the research process along within the organization in the face of inertia, resistance, misunderstanding, and other interfering and inhibiting forces. The researcher may have to provide that momentum personally:

Researchers need to know how to put their ideas across. Our people have been able to sell research and to persuade staff to go along.

Researchers have to convince people that their work will be helpful in gaining time, more money, better service, or increased efficiency.

One senior research officer described characteristics of a member of his staff who was particularly successful in promoting utilization:

X has been able to use her personality to good advantage. Part of it is charisma, and the other part is hard work. She is young, attractive, and outgoing. People see her as down-to-earth. She has no snobbish airs and graces. At the same time, she is clear-sighted, energetic, determined, and can apply a lot of muscle, if necessary.

Sometimes, promotional activity can draw upon outside influences for support. One researcher made known requests from outside universities and government bureaus for certain internal reports. This extra legitimation was employed to back up the efforts of the research section to have these reports acted upon. Several respondents indicated that consistency in the system of internal policies is required as an aspect of promoting research. Successful communication is not a one-dimensional process of routinely sending and receiving messages.

The place of promotional activity has been discussed by others. In addition to interpretation, Davis and Salasin (1975: 646) make a case for a more forceful approach:

> Persuasion may be used. Its success depends on the ability of the persuader to convince others that the rewards of the change counterbalance or outweigh the reasons for resistance.

Pellegrin (1965) concludes from his analysis that unless educational researchers take more forthright action in persuading teachers of the usefulness of empirical findings, research will be of limited effectiveness in the educational field. Rogers and Shoemaker (1971: 234) conclude from their exhaustive study of research on diffusion of innovations that one of the crucial variables in adoption of new methods is the amount of effort extended by the agent of diffusion; i.e., taking "an active rather than a passive role in the change process." Utilization is more likely to come about if the potential user can be convinced that there is a "relative advantage" to doing something new as compared to continuing as usual. And Patton et al. (1977: 159) observed that the greatest degree of active application of the evaluative studies they reviewed took place when evaluators were personally "committed to seeing their findings utilized."

UTILIZATION OF RESEARCH IS FACILITATED BY EFFECTIVE USE OF WRITTEN COMMUNICATION

In the previous sections we have described how direct interpersonal communication can be used with profit to form appropriate social-psychological links between researchers and practitioners. Respondents indicated that written communication also serves to affect the quality of attitudes and working relationships between these two sets of organizational actors. This aspect will be gone into in considerable detail in the next chapter, which deals with written reports. Here we will merely state the proposition in a cursory manner.

Respondents indicated use of a wide variety of media and approaches in transmitting written messages. These included newsletters, digests of research with explicit application suggestions, interim progress reports providing feedback during the course of a study, and final study reports presented in brief fashion — such as a concise memo with a summarizing diagram. A general strategic point of view about written communication emerged from one respondent:

> Don't overload busy managers and practitioners with written materials. Be selective about written reports. Make the reports as brief as possible and send different kinds of materials to different relevant people.

Other comments about content, form, and style of written communication are presented in the next chapter along with relevant information from the literature.

Facilitating Behavior by Operational People

We will shift at this point to those comments that were geared to operational people. Here the majority of comments were directed toward the chief administrative officer. This can be explained by the fact that the occupant of that position holds the greatest share of power and authority in the organization. Also, the role involves a benign overview of organizational functions and a stake in bringing them into proper alignment. These were apparently implicit assumptions of the interviewees, as managers were much in the limelight compared to their organizational subordinates with regard to affecting the research picture.

UTILIZATION OF RESEARCH IS FACILITATED WHEN MANAGERS CREATE AN ATMOSPHERE THAT IS FRIENDLY TO RESEARCH

It was suggested that the manager can be instrumental in subtle ways in creating an atmosphere that is friendly to research and researchers. The point is that certain values and conditions of work are more hospitable to the appreciation of research functions. Various aspects of such an atmosphere were identified:

Self-Examination

Our manager is continually educating himself to the value of research. He is willing to be convinced by authentic facts and demonstrates that he is prepared to accept criticism. He establishes a lot of informal contacts with staff throughout the organization where he tries to model this value. Basically, he attempts to motivate people to engage in self-examination.

Maximizing Service

I try to convey to the staff the notion of continual improvement in productivity. All of us have to work together as a team to improve services to the public, taking advantage of all contributions in the organization. The overriding consideration is maximum service to clients at the lowest feasible cost to the community.

Professional Pride

In my dealings with staff, I try to encourage a professional attitude — examine your premises, seek out new knowledge to improve your performance. I continually ask, "How can we, as professionals, do this job better?"

Open Communication

The agency has an ethos in favor of communication. Our manager is open-minded and change oriented. He uses an open form of management, sharing problems and issues with the staff. He is willing to listen to people and involve others in decision-making.

Rationality

Our organization needs a legitimate basis for decision-making. The borough council emphasizes this and respects research information in deciding how financial allocations will be made. I have a strong commitment to forward planning and to research as a rational tool in guiding that planning.

These general attitudinal attributes of managers have been noted by others. Davis and Salasin (1975) state that certain perspectives on the part of the leader of an organization can lead to its being more flexible and progressive. Among these they include: accepting risks, encouraging self-renewal on the part of oneself and others, focusing on substantive goals, and being an innovator oneself. Brown (1976) reports that "openness" on the part of managers was one of the main variables' associated with research utilization in a community mental health setting. Openness implies a willingness to expose uncertainties or deficiencies and a tendency to seek out actively new information. Glaser (1973) likewise found that one of the chief facilitating forces that bears on successful planned change in organizations is the presence of a leader with openness. From a broader perspective, Paisley (1969) shows that the cultural norms that are part of a "knowledge system environment" profoundly affect the workings and output of the knowledge system.

UTILIZATION OF RESEARCH IS FACILITATED WHEN MANAGERS OPENLY ADVOCATE AND INTERPRET THE VALUES OF RESEARCH IN THE ORGANIZATION

The research staff has a prime role in research promotion in the organization, but it can use help. Our informants indicate that help provided by agency managers has been critical in various settings. In addition to providing a background set of attitudes and values that are consistent with the values of research, it is useful for management to convey to operational people direct attitudinal support for research. This has already been discussed and illustrated in another connection in the chapter on structural factors. An aspect of this is the development by the director of formal policies and directives whose effect is to provide normative support for research.

UTILIZATION OF RESEARCH IS FACILITATED WHEN MANAGERS PROVIDE PSYCHIC SUPPORT TO RESEARCHERS

Being a researcher in a large organization devoted to the delivery of services can be a lonely circumstance. This sense of isolation, of being undervalued, not only affects the morale of researchers, but it can cause reactions of resentment, frustration, and superiority that work against positive relationships. This was keenly recognized by several of the managers. It was their opinion that the manager is in a key position to play an ameliorative role:

Researchers are not likely to get recognition either from other agency people or from the academic community. They are in an isolated position. Managers must make their research staff feel that they are being listened to — that their work is important and appreciated.

Research staff can easily feel that policy-making is taking place without the use of research evidence. It is important that managers show that they respect research, give it proper attention, and take it into account in working through their decisions.

UTILIZATION OF RESEARCH IS FACILITATED WHEN MANAGERS STEER RESEARCHERS INTO PARTICIPATION IN DECISION-MAKING PROCESSES

We have discussed the benefits of researchers having interpersonal contacts within the organization. Sometimes the road is blocked. Managers can help clear the way. Sometimes researchers themselves do not recognize the need for contact. Managers can provide the stimulus. (The previous chapter on structural factors discussed the usefulness of participation by researchers in management meetings, planning committees, and meetings in the operating divisions.) As one respondent observed: "managers should make it their business to include researchers in management group meetings." This provides not only structural linkage among different agency functions, but interpersonal linkage between different agency functionaries as well.

UTILIZATION OF RESEARCH IS FACILITATED WHEN MANAGERS KEEP RESEARCHERS FOCUSED ON SPECIFIC ORGANIZATIONAL PROBLEMS

We have discussed the socialization and training of researchers that press in the theoretical and technical direction. Researchers can easily lose sight of the operations research role they are to play in organizational settings. The prestige and reward system of their primary source of professional identification reinforces a broader, more abstract intellectual bearing. This works against optimal relationships that are conducive to application of research.

Managers can assist this by keeping researchers on the track, reminding them of the main problems and decisional issues that research should be addressing:

> Managers should be very critical of their research people. They should ask, "What does this study mean for this borough?"

Another researcher felt that research studies are most beneficial when they produce short-run payoffs to some segment of the agency. Practical, problem-related results can bring forth friendly and appreciative reactions by operational staff. The manager can play a role indirectly in bringing this about.

UTILIZATION OF RESEARCH IS FACILITATED WHEN MANAGERS SEE TO THE CONTINUITY OF RESEARCH STAFF

Several respondents spoke to the usefulness of reasonable longevity by research staff members. A high turnover rate interferes with progression in research studies. It also disrupts the pattern of relationships that is established between researchers and operational staff. As there is a certain delicacy in the quality of such relationships, and considerable time may be involved in forming them, it is a wise policy for managers to hold researchers in place for ample periods of time. This can be accomplished in part through the kind of psychic recognition mentioned earlier. To this should be added financial rewards, equipment and accommodations considered important by researchers, arrangements whereby researchers can participate in their discipline, and so on.

One seasoned manager with a deep commitment to integration of social research into social practice explicated what was apparently a general viewpoint. He placed the responsibility for better rapport squarely on the shoulders of researchers. Operational people, he felt, are pinned down to the job by manifold demands coming from clients, administrators, interest groups, government bureaus, and their professional disciplines. Researchers will be obliged to take the first steps in demonstrating the relevance of research to their work. He saw no gain in presenting practitioners with further demands to fill out additional forms and to change their customary procedures.

There were no villains or heroes in his scenario. Rather, our informant tried to present an objective, sympathetic understanding of the dynamics of the situation as he perceived it. He acknowledged that researchers and practitioners were dedicated professionals, doing valuable work under hampering difficulties; but, taking full account of the circumstances involved, the mandate for amelioration fell primarily on the one party rather than on the other.

AN APPLICATION CHECKLIST FOR ATTITUDINAL AND RELATIONAL FACTORS

Researchers Receiving Communication

☐ Are researchers attentive to the concerns and interests of operational people?

☐ Do researchers actively listen by drawing operational people out and/or being alert to informal clues of difficulties?

☐ Do researchers employ a manner that conveys respect and helpfulness?

☐ Do researchers exhibit interest in, and gain information about, the specific work tasks in which operational people are engaged?

☐ Are researchers mindful of "how the organization works," including factions, power blocs, and loci of decision-making?

Researchers Initiating Communication

- [ ] Do researchers have an affirmative style in extending themselves to people on the operational side?
- [ ] Do researchers associate personally with operational people by moving around in the environs of operations?
- [ ] Do researchers take part in agency meetings of various kinds that involve operational people, both meetings that focus on research and that are of a more general nature?
- [ ] Do researchers use communication that is interpretive and informative — explaining, illustrating, and demonstrating?
- [ ] Do researchers indicate support of positive features of existing practices and suggest changes in a manner that minimizes threat?
- [ ] When necessary, do researchers engage in active persuasion, "selling" people on the usefulness of following through on the implications of research?
- [ ] Do researchers make use of a sufficient, although not excessive, variety of written communications of different types for different audiences?

For Administrators

- [ ] Do administrators espouse and model general values supportive of research and its utilization, including such values as self-scrutiny, maximizing effective service, rationality, and open communication?
- [ ] Do administrators serve as advocates of research in the organization through personal expression and formal policy statements and directives?
- [ ] Do administrators provide psychic support to researchers through expression of appreciation of their efforts, and do they manifest use of research products in administrative and planning decisions?
- [ ] Do administrators seek to make researchers feel an integral part of the organization to counteract their potential sense of isolation?
- [ ] Do administrators encourage and facilitate the par-

ticipation of researchers in the group life and administrative processes of the organization?

☐ Do administrators help researchers to focus on operational problems of the organization?

☐ Do administrators make operational staff aware of the ways in which research has been helpful to them and in this way make friends for researchers in the organiztion?

☐ Do administrators attempt to provide for continuity of research staff as a way to sustain established relationships, offering appropriate incentives to researchers, and allowing means for them to continue to make contributions to their discipline?

This concludes the treatment of social-psychological variables from what could be gleaned from the interview data. In the chapter that follows, a particular form of communication, written reports, will come under scrutiny. It will quickly become obvious that there is more variation in the potential structure and texture of research reports than many researchers recognize and that these variations in reports may have a more profound differential effect upon their fate than is commonly appreciated.

REFERENCES

BECKHARD, RICHARD (1974) "ABS in health care systems: who needs it?" Journal of Applied Behavioral Science 10: 43-106.

BRIGHT, J. R. (1964) Research, Development, and Technological Innovation: An Introduction. Homewood, IL: Irwin.

BROWN, TIMOTHY (1976) "Guidelines for integrating program evaluation with administrative decision-making." Presented at APA Convention, Washington, DC.

CAPLAN, NATHAN (1977) "A minimal set of conditions necessary for the utilization of social science knowledge in policy formulation at the national level," pp. 183-197 in Carol H. Weiss (ed.) Using Social Research in Public Policy Making. Lexington, MA: D. C. Heath.

CHURCHMAN, C. WEST (1964) "Managerial acceptance of scientific recommendation." California Management Review 7, 1: 31-38.

COLEMAN, J. S., E. KATZ, and H. MENZEL (1966) Medical Innovations: A Diffusion Study. Indianapolis: Bobbs-Merrill.

COOPER, C. R. and B. ARCHAMBAULT [eds.] (1968) Communication, Dissemination, and Utilization of Research Information in Rehabilitation Counseling. Proceedings of a regional conference sponsored by the Department of Guidance and Psychological Services. Springfield, MA: Springfield College (in collaboration with Rehabilitation Service Administration, Department of Health, Education, and Welfare).

CRANE, D. (1970) "The nature of scientific communication and influence." International Social Science Journal 1: 28-41.

DAVIS, HOWARD and SUSAN SALASIN (1975) "The utilization of evaluation," pp. 621-666 in Elmer Struening and Marcia Guttentag (eds.) Handbook of Evaluation Research, Vol. 1. Beverly Hills, CA: Sage.

DONNISON, DAVID (1972) "Research for policy." Minerva 10, 4: 519-536.

EASH, M. J. (1968) "Bringing research findings into classroom practice." Elementary School Journal 68, 8: 410-418.

GLASER, EDWARD M. (1973) "Knowledge transfer and institutional change." Professional Psychology 4: 434-444.

HAVELOCK, RONALD G. (1969) Planning for Innovation Through Dissemination and Utilization of Knowledge. Ann Arbor: Center for Research on Utilization of Scientific Knowledge, Institute for Social Research, University of Michigan.

——— (1968) "Dissemination and translation roles," pp. 64-119 in T. L. Eidell and J. M. Kitchel (eds.) Knowledge Production and Utilization in Educational Administration. Eugene: Center for the Advanced Study of Educational Administration, University of Oregon.

KOGAN, L. S. (1963) "The utilization of social work research," Social Casework 44: 569-574.

PAISLEY, WILLIAM J. (1969) "Perspectives on the utilization of knowledge." Presented at the meeting of the American Educational Research Association, Los Angeles, February.

——— (1968) "Information needs and uses," pp. 1-30 in C. A. Cuadra (ed.) Annual Review of Information Science and Technology, Vol. 3. New York: Interscience.

PARKER, E. B. and W. J. PAISLEY (1966) "Research for psychologists on the interface of the scientist and his information system." American Psychologist 21: 1060-1071.

PATTON, MICHAEL Q. et al (1977) "In search of impact: an analysis of the utilization of federal health evaluation research," pp. 141-163 in Carol H. Weiss (ed.) Using Social Research in Public Policy Making. Lexington, MA: D. C. Heath.

PELLEGRIN, RONALD J. (1965) "The place of research in planned change," pp. 65-75 in R. O. Carlson et al., Change Processes in the Public Schools. Eugene: Center for the Advanced Study of Educational Administration, University of Oregon.

PELZ, DONALD C. and FRANK M. ANDREWS (1976) Scientists in Organizations: Productive Climates for Research and Development. Ann Arbor: Institute for Social Research, University of Michigan.

POSER, E. G., I. DUNN, and R. M. SMITH (1964) "Resolving conflicts between clinical and research teams." Mental Hospitals 15, 5: 278-282.

ROGERS, EVERETT M. (1967) "Communication of vocational rehabilitation innovations," pp. 19-32 in Communication, Dissemination and Utilization of Rehabilitation Research Information. Studies in Rehabilitation Counselor Training No. 5. Washington, DC: Joint Liaison Committee of the Council of State Administrators of Vocational Rehabilitation and Rehabilitation Counselor Educators, Department of Health, Education, and Welfare.

——— and E. F. SHOEMAKER (1971) Communication of Innovations: A Cross-Cultural Approach. New York: Macmillan.

ROSE, RICHARD (1977) "Disciplined research and undisciplined problems," pp. 23-25 in Carol H. Weiss (ed.) Using Social Research in Public Policy Making. Lexington, MA: D. C. Heath.

SWANSON, DON R. (1966) "On improving communications among scientists." Bulletin of the Atomic Scientists 22, 2: 8-12.

VAN den BAN, ANNE W. (1963) "Utilization and publication of findings," in C. H. Backstrom and G. D. Hursh (eds.) Survey Resarch Methods in Developing Nations. Chicago: Northwestern University.

WILSON, ELMO C. (1961) "The application of social research findings," pp. 47-58 in Case Studies in Bringing Behavioral Science into Use: Studies in the Utilization of Behavioral Science, Vol. 1. Palo Alto, CA: Institute for Communication Research, Stanford University.

Chapter 5

REPORTS AND PRODUCTS OF RESEARCH

It is true, alas, as Havelock (1969) observes, that research knowledge for the most part is read primarily by other researchers. When the objective is the furtherance of scientific endeavor, this pattern is advantageous. When the objective is the enhancement of practice performance, it can be a disaster.

The form into which the results of research are placed may have an important impact on the way the research is received and whether it is applied subsequently in agency programs and operations. The term "products" is used in the title of this section in order to convey the idea that research presentations can be made in other than a formal statistical display or analysis. Sets of detailed recommendations may be included. Qualitative and illustrative materials may be relied upon. Practical operational guides based on research findings may be distributed. Multiple types of presentation may be prepared for different constituencies within the organization. Respondents interviewed in this study had much to say about research reports and what made them subject to serious consideration or prompt dismissal on the part of operational people. Their comments cover a range of dimensions of the subject.

UTILIZATION OF RESEARCH IS FACILITATED BY RESEARCH REPORTS THAT ARE RELEVANT TO AGENCY PROBLEMS AND CONCERNS

Perhaps the most commonly expressed view of respondents was that research reports need to be tailored to address real and compelling problems that agency administrators and practitioners are forced to deal with. For many of those interviewed, the fundamental legitimacy of the research function was bound up in this notion of practice or program relevancy:

> Information is often presented to us in a way that is too broad, not sufficiently precise or relevant to deal with specific agency problems. It is not practical or related to actions we can take.
> Researchers need to communicate directly in a way that is related to real problems. It is true that theoretical writings and broad research are necessary, but we also need very practical writings and studies.

The latter observer felt that there needs to be a division of labor; i.e., broader research endeavors should be reserved for the university setting, and agency research should focus on practical matters. When research reports do not illuminate agency problems in this kind of practical way, they were often seen as intellectual playthings of a dilettante staff absorbed in their personal, esoteric preoccupations.

Weiss (1977: 4) concludes from her investigations that for applied people, relevance is a primary consideration. "First, a study had to be relevant to the work they were doing. If it was not, it didn't get into the ball park. They were simply uninterested." From our interviews it appears that relevance can be viewed from a number of different angles.

Specific Recommendations Pointing
to Action Steps

A considerable number of respondents insisted that research reports need to make clear and specific the programmatic implications of the study findings. Several comments convey this sense:

> You need to know what to do about what you find out.
> The study should be specific and responsive to the problem.
> One study that was used well in our situation came up with a set of answers that responded to the problem we were concerned about. It made a good case for specific action.
> Research studies should make explicit recommendations.
> Researchers can lose their credibility by not making clear the action implications of their work.

One way of achieving a fairly concrete level of application relevance is to have the initial findings reviewed by a selected group of operational people who are among the natural ultimate users of the materials. This group can both assess the findings and work through some procedural possibilities for the application setting. When the research report is distributed more broadly, it would, in this way, contain both the perspectives of researchers, who are concerned with "truth," and of operational people, who are concerned with "action."

These results are confirmed elsewhere. Based on observing utilization of social welfare research, Klein (1968) indicates the process is facilitated when implications are stated in clear cause-and-effect statements. Also, basing his observations on the social welfare context, Benjamin (1972: 19-20) states that the research worker

> has got to be prepared to fill out the picture behind the figures, including all the deficiencies and reservations. He has got to be able to indicate where the figures appear to lead in

terms of policy implications, and he has got to be able to do this in a simple and direct manner.

According to Weiss (1977), administrators ordinarily apply a "utilization test" to information. Does the research provide a direction for feasible change? Wilson (1961) found that one of the main causes of failure to use research was absence of comparative cost estimates for various recommendations or estimates of the length of time required for implementation.

Short-Term Time Perspective and Situational Concreteness

It was felt by respondents that problem relevance is aided by studies with short-term ramifications, tied to concrete agency situations. As one executive stated it:

> Research is not often enough related to the here and now. Some immediate, short-run successes are needed in order to add to the researchers' legitimacy in the agency.

As stated by a researcher, "Researchers have to have some friends in the organization, and showing short-run payoffs is a way to accomplish this." An executive related the point to his ability to maintain his own acceptance in the agency. He felt that he must be able to justify expenses for research and, thus, to maintain support for such expenditures on the basis that at least *some* segment of the agency feels a short-term benefit from most of the studies conducted.

Two different views on how to accomplish this result were expressed. A researcher with a fairly large program indicated that an ample number of research staffers is needed. In this way the unit can conduct some longer-term, substantial projects and still have the manpower capability to respond immediately to problems requiring quick answers. In her view, a balance of long-term and short-term undertakings is useful. A sufficient number of staff provides the room to maneuver to achieve the proper balance. She warns against overdoing large projects that extend over time because a certain number of short-term, responsive projects are necessary as a tradeoff for the more substantial studies to be carried out. Another researcher, with a managerial, operations research outlook, took the view that the time scale of *all* studies should be short term, efficiently and tightly scheduled, in-house in character, with acceptance of the idea of working quickly, and a consciousness of programmatic impact.

It has been pointed out elsewhere that policy makers also value information that incorporates long-term indicators and provides estimates of trends (Rich, 1975). The two factors are not necessarily in conflict. Managers may likewise appreciate trend data but feel pressed more than policy makers to have information of greater immediacy available, at hand, in order to cope with day-to-day operations. Concerning situational concreteness, applicability to a specific local area, according to Klein (1968), is highly conducive to research utilization. Van de Vall and his associates (1976) found primary data from the concrete application setting to be facilitative of utilization.

Conserving or Increasing Agency Resources

From managers, in particular, came the view that research studies are especially appreciated when they conserve the resource base of the agency. Several respondents suggested that research is helpful when it "helps save money" or "takes pressures off the organization" or "facilitates better use of resources within existing agency limitations":

> Very often research findings imply expansion of manpower or increases in cost to provide new services. A continuous series of such studies can cause serious problems for management.

Conversely:

> More time should be spent in seeing how good ideas can be
> used, despite economic constraints. In other words, can
> necessary changes be considered with an eye on low-cost pro-
> grams?

These managers are saying that researchers should conduct
their work with awareness and appreciation of the agency
financial realities rather than with a romantic attachment to
objectivity.

Adding to resources, as well as conserving them, was a pronounced theme. One researcher portrayed his program as
highly successful and respected in the organization because its
"recommendations have brought good news by giving us additional resources."

It was pointed out that resource benefits of research should
be interpreted to two important constituencies of the agency:

> *Practitioners/field staff:* Show field people the utility of fac-
> tual information in helping to obtain money and increase
> staff, and to relieve pressures on them.
> *Top policy group:* Sell the research to committees and of-
> ficers of the [city or area] council by pointing out its advan-
> tages in bringing about economic savings and concrete ser-
> vices that are politically attractive.

In the view of Benjamin (1972: 19), one of the most important functions of the research staff in the social services field
is protecting the supply of resources. He states:

> We have to begin by making an inventory of all these
> resources, both statutory and voluntary, looking not only at
> the way they are disposed but at the way in which their size and
> disposition may be influenced. What is the expectation for in-
> creasing them or altering their distributions? What social and
> economic factors within the environment might affect them?

Legitimating Existing Programs —
Pointing to Needed Change

An additional criterion of relevance of research, expressed especially by managers, is that it legitimate existing program directions of the agency. For example, one respondent spoke of research "confirming a need" that agency services were aimed at. Directors experience a great number of pressures, many of them contradictory, from different quarters. They also have self-doubts about what they (and their organization) are doing, given the lack of firm theory and hard data in the human service fields. Because of the volume and diversity of demands, it is easier, operationally, to keep to current programming rather than to make shifts. Consequently, research that gives support to existing programs is particularly reassuring.

A counterpart theme was also expressed, perhaps not as frequently, by both directors and researchers: Research should be change oriented. As one respondent put it:

> Research should not be seen as only providing responsive information to administratively defined problems, it should also serve as a change force in the organization.

To this respondent, who held a research position that also involved strong program planning components, the research unit needs to function as a "subversive element" in the agency — raising painful issues, puncturing held beliefs, and, pressing for new directions of service.

Relevance of research was, thus, defined both in terms of confirmation and nullification of established programs and methods. While these views are in overt conflict, they appear to reflect a valid duality concerning how research is viewed and the functions it can perform in serving the purposes of the agency.

Weiss (1977) discovered a similar tension in the subjects she interviewed. In applying the "utility test" for a research study, they indicated two criteria: (1) *challenge to the status quo* (does the research challenge current programs and policies and provide a direction for change?) and, (2) *action orientation* (does the research deal with feasible changes in things that feasibly can be changed?). The issue may be viewed politically. For a manager, confirmation of current programming can be comforting information and a politically useful weapon for obtaining increased funds, squelching dissident staff, and so on. At the same time, failure to shift in time to changing environmental conditions can result in serious organizational problems, reflect on his or her judgment, and affect his or her standing in the organization and community. While both these factors were present, our interviews leaned in the direction of legitimation rather than change. This is consistent with Rich's (1975: 241) observation that often "information is collected in order to support a policy position already taken."

UTILIZATION OF RESEARCH IS FACILITATED BY RESEARCH REPORTS THAT EXHIBIT CREDIBILITY

While practicality and utility of research received the bulk of emphasis, an additional theme reflected prominently in the interviews was that the report should not give the appearance of being technically suspect. Its methodology should not be subject to criticism, and it should manifest sufficient objectivity to be convincing.

Some of those interviewed considered the question of scientific validity to be a proper and important consideration in its own right; for example, a view that the manager needs authentic information in order to make rational decisions. Others saw this in a more political way:

> Prove the validity of the study and be careful in the conduct of the research. This will allow you to sell the research more readily.

Provide sufficient information to managers about the research program and its results so they are clear about this and can convince others, including members of the [city or area] council.

It was brought out by several of the respondents that studies often signal increased funding by the political sponsoring group, the council. This group wants to be convinced that a designated need is real, that it has been demonstrated in a technically sound way sufficient to justify the allocation of scarce funds being sought by parties with conflicting claims. Certain findings may require practitioners to change accustomed ways of work or to take additional responsibilities. They want to be sure that these extra demands on them are totally justified and that the service implications are safe for clients.

One researcher acknowledged that, often, methods involve compromise techniques and results are less than definitive. In her view it is inappropriate for the researcher simply to pass over gross uncertainty to operational people. This is highly confusing and leads to a disenchantment with research. These individuals are already coping with great amounts of uncertainty. This respondent felt that "the researcher should absorb as much of the uncertainty as possible himself." By this she meant that the researcher should follow through in an educative fashion, advising people in a clear way about both limitations and strengths of the data, suggesting where risks more justifiably may be taken, and plugging up holes with findings from other studies or related field experiences elsewhere. Validity, in short, should be treated in a way that is organizationally sensitive rather than merely technically correct.

Another aspect of credibility/validity brought out in the interviews went to the matter of comprehensiveness of reports. This implies a sufficient amount of information and a rounded document. Regarding a study that was judged to have had a clear impact on the agency:

> The report came up with a set of answers that was broadly responsive to the problem. It made a complete case; nothing else was needed. It was well written, persuasive, and stood on its own merits.

Credibility, therefore, includes validity from a technical standpoint, but seems also related to the form of presentation: its sense of being complete, authoritative, convincing, and well informed concerning the general issue under study.

Other studies and writings are consistent with these results. Weiss (1977) found in her investigation that research used by human service administrators was subjected by them to a "truth test"; i.e., was the research trustworthy, can it be relied upon, was it produced through appropriate scientific procedures? Her subjects applied two main criteria to assessing the accuracy of a study. One was *research quality*, which included validity, internal consistency, objectivity, and so on. The other was conforming to the *users' experience* and "sense of the situation." Both pertained to *trusting* a research study. Paisley (1968) indicates that the technical quality of the information source is of importance to engineering professionals in determining whether they will employ new findings. It is pointed out by Smith et al. (1969), however, that the details of research do not need to be presented per se. In reviewing their experience in a Vocational Rehabilitation Research Utilization Laboratory, Soloff et al. (1975) state that practitioners were deeply concerned with whether a research-derived prescription "will work," and that their tendency to use it was increased by "awareness of other people's positive experience" with it. Davis and Salasin (1975: 64) indicate that credibility may stem from "soundness of evidence" or from "espousal by highly respected persons or institutions."

UTILIZATION OF RESEARCH IS FACILITATED BY A STYLE OF PRESENTATION THAT COMMUNICATES WITH POTENTIAL USERS IN THE AGENCY SYSTEM

From the comments that were made, it is evident that the style of presentation of research is a troubling element within many operating organizations. Researchers appear in their training to be socialized to write in technical language suited to other researchers, a form that is either offensive or incomprehensible to many of the audiences and constituencies within service organizations. The character of presentation of reports received a great deal of commentary, both in terms of what is typically wrong with them and what can be done to improve them.

Language Simplicity

"Obfuscated language," "too much jargon," "too detailed" were some of the phrases used to describe many research reports, attributes that were seen as inhibiting their utilization. From virtually everyone interviewed came the opinion that reports should be written in simpler language and in terms that are understandable to operational people:

> Researchers need to translate complex ideas and technical language into language that is familiar to managers.
> Reports often have too much detail and the language is too difficult. The writers should try to simplify and summarize, maybe using graphs or a simple rank order of important points.

All the criticism did not fall on the researchers. A manager stated that blame flows in both directions. In his view, while researchers should put things at a level comfortable to operational people, "managers should take more responsibility to understand and appreciate research." This respondent felt that managers are too often frightened of statistics and do not equip themselves to deal with research in a way required to manage organizations scientifically in the contemporary scene.

This problem of distinct languages in the culture of science and the culture of practice has been pointed out by many observers. Coleman et al. (1966) found that for medical practitioners there was too much information, often spelled out in too highly specialized an idiom, too ambiguously, or in technical language that obstructs its flow to individuals who could make practical use of it.

Soloff et al. (1975) speak to the utility of "highly readable prose," presented in a form that is "visually attractive and clearly written." In concurrence, Davis and Salasin (1975) declare for "ease of presentation" that is facilitated by "readability, coherence and understanding" from the standpoint of the intended audience. Van den Ban (1963) devoted considerable space to a discussion of writing style, diagrams, tables, and other visual aids. In comments reported later, respondents indicate how this can be accomplished.

Brevity

A common complaint was that reports are often too lengthy. The ambience in all organizations that were visited was harried, pressured, and turbulent. Operational staff repeatedly spoke of "client bombardment." Leisure time for extended reading was virtually nonexistent. As one individual commented, "Lengthy reports are a hindrance — people don't know what to do with them." Recurrently, those interviewed called for reports that are brief, concise, terse, and to the point.One suggested a "short, snappy memo with a diagram," another, "use of information summaries." Even when the body of the report is substantial, it was recommended that a concise summary of the essence be placed in a prominent place. The following is a typical point of view:

Information should be presented in brief form. There should be a clear, encapsulated summary of findings and recommendations. If possible, the summary should be no more than a page.

A large number of researchers and observers have commented upon the need to present research implications in a way that accommodates the mind-set and situation of practitioners. Brevity, speed of access, and the packaging of relatively small units of information are called for by Magisos (1971) and Paisley (1968). The chances of impact are increased, according to Glaser et al. (1969), if the findings are presented in brief and nontechnical form. Smith et al. (1969) point to the value of selecting and interpreting the research with an application focus and mainly within the context of clarification and illustration.

Attractiveness-Evocativeness

A report must grab the eye of the prospective reader. In the hustling atmosphere of human services work many pieces of paper beseech the attention of operational people. Heaped up "in-baskets" and cluttered desks are common. Unless particular items have the quality of a "command performance" (mandated responses required by supervisors in the chain of command), they must compete with one another to be noticed. A respondent recalled that a report failed to gain action because

it wasn't dramatic enough. The standards of the presentation may have been at the wrong level.

On the other hand, other reports were described as successful because they "gave a visual impression," "caught the human side," or "made an excellent presentation with recommendations that were dramatic." Picturesque language seemed to be part of what is required, but also the use of pictorial methods — graphs, charts, illustrations, color highlights, and the like. For the researcher the message is to heed the packaging of the product in addition to the quality of its contents.

Davis and Salasin (1975: 641) recommended the use of "pictorial and other illustrative material." The beneficial effects of qualitative data and presentations are pointed out in a study of research utilization in industrial settings (Van de Vall et al., 1976). Managers were found to be more likely to apply research in their work if a qualitative rather than a tabular form of presentation was made and if the methodological mix of research methods favored the qualitative ones.

Self-Contained Completeness

This was already touched upon in the validity section. It will be repeated in relation to presentation style. Respondents indicated that they wanted a rounded picture, one in which all the necessary elements were in place, each one treated briefly. Readers did not wish to be referred to other assorted documents and sources in order to get the full story. To the degree possible, they were asking for a presentation that is self-contained and "stands on its own two feet." There is a potential contradiction between the notions of brevity and of completeness. Apparently, what the interviewees were saying is that conciseness and ideational completeness are both useful, and that reports should strive to incorporate both features.

Self-containment has the sense of saving time in the same way that brevity does. If the full picture is presented in one place, extra time does not have to be expended in further inquiries and additional reading to round out the picture.

UTILIZATION OF RESEARCH IS FACILITATED BY REPORTS THAT ARE SENSITIVE TO PSYCHOLOGICAL DYNAMICS AND ORGANIZATIONAL POLITICS

It was generally agreed that researchers do not pay sufficient attention to human factors operating within the organizational environment. Quite often research findings convey implicit or explicit criticism of the functioning of particular individuals or particular groups in the organization. Various examples were given. New arrangements suggested by research may result in loss of status or authority by certain members of the organization or in a disruption of customary and comfortable ways of doing things. When this kind of information is presented in a brusk manner, it frequently evokes resistance on the part of those affected, causing them to dig in their heels rather than open their minds. Those interviewed felt that researchers should be attuned to such human and organizational dynamics and prepared to present themselves and their reports in such a way as to minimize oppositional reflexes:

> Researchers should know how to play the political game to achieve their objectives. You have to know how to get your findings across with an awareness of the implications of implementation.

Being attuned to the social context means also knowing how to impact those in the organization who are in a position to move the situation along, even in the face of opposition:

> You have to sell the research to significant individuals in the department, such as top committees and officers. You need to underline to them the advantages, such as economic savings and practical gains.

A manager of a large department containing a substantial research program made the interesting point that researchers need to be sensitive and at the same time determined. Psychological and organizational acumen was not viewed as dampening a commitment to forward thrust:

> Researchers must find a better way of getting across their criticisms. They have to be sensitive to people's feelings, but at the same time sell their research findings in an aggressive way. I am not asking them to back off, rather to go forward in an assertive but feeling way.

This is a difficult balance to achieve. It may take more than most researchers are equipped to handle. The implication is clear, however, that preparation for this type of research should involve such training. The psychological issue has been put in a nutshell by Van den Ban (1963: 19):

> In order to be able to work with enthusiasm a good practitioner should be convinced that his work is important and that the way he does it is basically correct. A good scientist, on the other hand, has the task to question this, which might make the practitioner uncomfortable and defensive.

Glaser and Wrenn (1966) assert that changes are accepted in direct proportion to which potential users recognize that their self-interest is benefited by the change. A wide-ranging discussion of psychological and organizational variables can be found in Davis and Salasin (1975). Their model of utilization attempts to "recognize the humanness of the participants involved" and includes such factors as the following: sympathy with the user is indicated; potential benefits are made clear; risks are surfaced and discussed; objections are taken account of and dealt with promptly; and essential information is reiterated at appropriate intervals. All these techniques would appear to be responsive to the issues raised by those who were interviewed in the study.

UTILIZATION OF RESEARCH IS FACILITATED
BY MULTIPLE FORMS OF REPORTING
TAILORED TO DIFFERENT AUDIENCES AND PURPOSES

This point reappears once again. Just as researchers are often wedded to one style of writing, they tend to visualize a single version of a research report for transmitting information. Respondents claimed that this was an erroneous and limiting vision. They insisted that different forms of reporting are appropriate vehicles for different audiences:

> I had two forms of the survey, one for officials and another for public meetings.

> In the report of the study there was a separate, short, management version, emphasizing the recommendations.

> We had an original report and a summary form for the field staff. This was more gimmicky and included the forms that were recommended for use by practitioners in the future. Seeing what the forms actually looked like made the field staff less apprehensive.

> We found it best to break up the report and present it in a series of magazine pieces.

> Our main document was available for anyone to look at, but we divided it into a series of smaller reports. Different reports went to the statistics committee, the personnel committee, and the social services committee of the council.

Other factors were mentioned as well. These included the quality of the paper, its color, and expansiveness of writing style. All should be considered in communicating to particular target audiences. A pose of austerity might be best for some.

Some respondents pointed to the relevance of different audiences for progress reports during the course of the research process. Not only did they feel there were different audiences for the final report but different audiences for interim reports as well:

It is important to give feedback during the various stages of the study. The final report is not the main thing and may almost be incidental if proper reporting to groups takes place along the way. They will have already become informed and psychologically invested in the outcome of the study.

Evidence from a variety of human service fields supports the results of these interviews. Writing from a community mental health perspective, Halpert (1966) indicates that specific audiences have to be identified and specialized materials prepared to focus on these audiences and on particular field problems. Magisos (1971) found that different categories of educators experienced different forms of information as being useful. It is stated by Smith and his associates (1969) that different materials should be prepared for school personnel with different roles and responsibilities. They also state that the appropriate vehicle for dissemination to practitioners should be a spelled-out program rather than basic findings and their implications. Before the final research findings are reported, according to Glaser and Taylor (1969), progress reports, discussion drafts, and other interim feedback should be provided to potential users. A particular technique along these lines is described by Chesler and Fox (1967), who met with the user group for purposes of planning jointly the means and mechanisms of reporting.

Intelligence from Roberts and Larsen (1971) and Carter (1968) tells us that, while good reports are vital, they should not be relied upon exclusively; other methods using interpersonal contact should supplement the report itself. In the Roberts and Larsen study the primary source of innovation was personal contact. Carter suggests use of intermediate personnel who can assist with communicating the researcher's findings to audiences of potential users.

Readers who are researchers in the field of communications will find this discussion of special audiences compatible with their theoretical outlook, and self-evident. Whether they ordinarily apply this knowledge in communicating their own work is a matter of less certainty. The results of this inquiry should prod researchers generally to heightened awareness of multiple audiences and to the need for differential reporting.

CONCLUSIONS ON RESEARCH REPORTS

The results presented here are generally compatible, with some variations, with the findings of Weiss (1977c). Her work was in the mental health field, concentrated on policy makers primarily, and was based on their reactions to sample study report summaries rather than on the actual use of research reports. Using a more rigorous statistical analysis than was attempted here, Weiss concludes that research reports are subjected to two main forms of appraisal: a truth test and a utility test. Each of these is further subdivided as follows:

Truth Test: Is the Research Trustworthy?
Research quality — was there use of appropriate scientific procedures?
Conformity with the user's expectations — does it agree with the decision maker's personal experience, knowledge, and values?

Utility Test: Is the Research Practical?
Challenge to the status quo — does the research challenge current philosophy, program, or practice? Does it offer alternative pictures of reality or general perspectives for modification?
Action orientation — does the research show how to make feasible changes in areas subject to feasible change?

These factors are included among those resulting from our study, together with several others that have appeared also to be worthy of note. Some variations in emphasis are of interest.

Weiss found challenge to the status quo to be of greater weight than it seemed to be among the managers with whom we consulted. This factor was indeed mentioned and given credence by our respondents, but they emphasized to a greater degree program support and careful, incremental change. This may be explained, perhaps, in two ways. The higher-level policy makers interviewed by Weiss may need to be more in touch with trends such as shifts in population, economic swings, or changes in political fashion than do the managers of local social service departments with whom we spoke. The policy maker's job may require him to be more finely tuned in responses to such social fluctuations, lest his or her professional judgment and political acumen be subject to criticism. Our managers and planners in local services worked within the parameters of established national social services policies. Their task was the efficient delivery of these services in keeping with the existing policies. For them, those things that facilitated delivery, rather than defined the basic character of the services, themselves, were of prime importance. Policy makers may appreciate challenge to a greater degree than managers. It may be more functional for them.

The second explanation for our divergence from Weiss relates to the question asked in our survey, "Which reports were *actually used* in planning your services, and what accounts for your having used them?" Her study dealt with potential use in a more artificial situation. "Provocative" reports may affect an applied person's thinking in a general and long-term way. "Practical" reports may affect actual behavior in a more immediate way. Our results focus on attributes of reports that may stimulate such immediate implemental effects.

With regard to Weiss's truth test, we would frame the issue slightly differently. The quality of the research (validity, objectivity) is seen as important by subjects in both studies. In addition, we found that applied people turn to what might be termed external corroborating evidence. This may involve their own experience and values (Weiss's conformity with user's expectations). It may also be based on the experience of other applied people, the word of respected authorities or institutions, even the views of influential community people, political figures, and so on. The external corroborating evidence from the field situation is broader than personal expectations. The broad view is important because the risk in acting upon presumed knowledge can be very high — damage to the physical or mental health of clients, great economic waste, organizational embarrassment resulting in loss of jobs, or political upheavals. The scientist puts his or her reputation on the line with a truth claim that could later be disproved. The norms of science, however, permit and even encourage such innovative grasps at truth in line with the experimental, empirical, trial-and-error character of the scientific method itself.

The applied person may have to be more rigorous and cautious than the scientist because the consequences of miscalculation in action may be more serious, widespread, and immediate. In addition, some of those consulted within his or her operational system can be made to absorb some of the risk, or at least be less vitriolic in pouncing on failures, if they have participated in the weighing of evidence. For this reason, a wide range of corroborating sources, beyond a personal response, are drawn upon and implicated in the judgment of truth and assessment of its application meaning.

AN APPLICATION CHECKLIST
FOR RESEARCH REPORTS AND PRODUCTS

In this section we will again construct a heuristic checklist of variables to be considered in preparing a report meant for use by applied professionals. The checklist might be used as a guide in outlining a report or as a tool for assessing a preliminary version. Not all items will be given equal weight; and, at this stage of theoretical development, the judgment of individuals intimately familiar with the particular utilization context is, perhaps, the best key to choice and emphasis among the items.

Relevance to Agency Problems and Concerns

Specificity and Action Orientation
- ☐ Are recommendations specific?
- ☐ Do they point to explicit action steps?
- ☐ Are they placed in the report so that they stand out?
- ☐ Have operational people reviewed the recommendations and provided implemental details?

Time and Place Concreteness
- ☐ Are short-term implications spelled out?
- ☐ Is the "here and now" agency situation emphasized?

Resource Considerations
- ☐ Does the report address the agency resource situation?
- ☐ Does it indicate possibilities of conserving or increasing agency resources through implementing recommendations?

Legitimating Existing Program;
Pointing to Needed Change
- ☐ Does the report legitimate or support programs or values that are important to the organization or its constituent groups?
- ☐ Does the report point to needed changes that would improve service or help the organization to cope more effectively with a changing environment?
- ☐ Does the report appreciate the existing program efforts?
- ☐ Does it minimize potential threat to organizational members in making changes?

Agency Practical Concerns
- ☐ Does the report clearly indicate how it is relevant to agency practical concerns?
- ☐ Is relevance to *problem solution* as well as to problem definition brought out concretely?

Credibility of the Report

Technical Adequacy and Objectivity

☐ Is the methodology of the study specified, explained, and justified (including limitations)?

☐ Is an objective posture projected (showing alternative interpretations, actions, implications, and so on)?

☐ Is uncertainty resolved by the writer to the greatest degree possible?

☐ Is the information substantively complete and rounded (in a concise way)?

☐ Can further confirmation of findings and recommendations be given (through other studies, experiences of operational people, support from respected individuals inside or outside the organization)?

Style of Presentation

Simplicity in Language Use

☐ Is the report written in direct, nontechnical terms and in an idiom familiar to intended users?

☐ Is the level of detail moderate (enough to provide intelligence, but not so much as to discourage the reader)?

☐ Are statistical terms and expositions kept to the minimum amount necessary?

☐ Are technical matters presented in a discursive and interpretive way when possible?

Brevity

☐ Is the report presented in a concise, economical fashion?

☐ Are time- and space-conserving techniques used (summary memo, synthesizing charts and diagrams, and so on)?

☐ Has the report been issued in several short pieces, if appropriate?

Attractiveness/Evocativeness

☐ Is the presentation written in a way that is appealing, interesting, or dramatic?

☐ Is it attractive in appearance?

- [ ] Is there use of specific features such as color, variation in format, pictures, illustrations, human interest vignettes?
- [ ] Is a general "packaging" concept involved in designing the presentation?

Completeness

- [ ] Does the presentation have sufficient breadth to give a comprehensive picture of the subject?
- [ ] Is there use of appendices and abstracts that relieve the reader of search for additional material or extensive supplementary reading?

Psychological and Organizational Dynamics

Psychological Sensitivity

- [ ] Is the report stated in a supportive way so as to mitigate defensive reactions to implied criticism?
- [ ] Are potential benefits and enlightened self-interest highlighted?
- [ ] Have those involved in implied changes been given an opportunity to comment and work through their feelings?
- [ ] Have gatekeepers and influentials been informed and prepared to interpret and support findings?

Multiple and Differential Reporting

- [ ] Have different reports been considered or prepared for different audiences and user groups, inside the organization and outside?
- [ ] Have interim or milestone reports been issued for different user groups?
- [ ] Have representatives of different user groups been consulted regarding what form of reporting would be preferred?
- [ ] Has interpersonal contact and communication been employed to supplement or reinforce written communication?

REFERENCES

BENJAMIN, BERNARD (1972) "Research strategies in social service departments of local authorities in Great Britain." Journal of Social Policy 2, 1: 13-26.

CARTER, LAUNOR F. (1968) "Knowledge production and utilization in contemporary organizations," pp. 1-20 in T. L. Eidell and J.M. Kitchel (eds.) Knowledge Production and Utilization in Educational Administration. Eugene: Center for the Advanced Study of Education Administration, University of Oregon.

CHESLER, MARK and R. FOX (1967) "Teacher peer relations and educational change." National Education Association Journal 56, 5: 25-26.

COLEMAN, J. S., E. KATZ, and H. MENZEL (1966) Medical Innovation: A Diffusion Study. Indianapolis: Bobbs-Merrill.

DAVIS, HOWARD and SUSAN SALASIN (1975) "The utilization of evaluation," pp. 621-666 in Elmer Struening and Marcia Guttentag (eds.) Handbook of Evaluation Research, Vol. I. Beverly Hills, CA: Sage.

GLASER, EDWARD M., H. S. COFFEE, J. B. MARKS, and I. B. SARASON (1967) Utilization of Applicable Research and Demonstration Results. Los Angeles: Human Interaction Research Institute.

GLASER, EDWARD and S. TAYLOR (1969) Factors Influencing the Success of Applied Research. Washington, DC: National Institute of Mental Health, Department of Health, Education, and Welfare.

GLASER, EDWARD and C. G. WRENN (1966) Putting Research, Experimental, and Demonstration Findings to Use. Washington, DC: Office of Manpower Policy, Evaluation and Research, U.S. Department of Labor.

HALPERT, HAROLD P. (1966) "Communication as a basic tool in promoting utilization of research findings." Community Mental Health Journal 2, 3: 231-236.

HAVELOCK, RONALD G. (1969) Planning for Innovation through Dissemination and Utilization of Knowledge. Ann Arbor: Center for Research on Utilization of Scientific Knowledge, Institute for Social Research, University of Michigan.

KLEIN, HELEN D. (1968) "The Missouri story: a chronicle of research utilization and program planning." Presented at the National Conference of Social Welfare.

KOGAN, L.S. (1963) "The utilization of social work research." Social Casework 44: 569-574.

MAGISOS, J. H. (1971) Interpretation of Target Audience Needs in the Design of Information Dissemination Systems for Vocational-Technical Education. Columbus: The Center for Vocational and Technical Education, Ohio State University.

PAISLEY, WILLIAM J. (1968) "Information needs and uses," pp. 1-30 in C. A. Cuadra (ed.) Annual Review of Information Science and Technology, Vol. 3. New York: Interscience.

RICH, ROBERT F. (1975) "Selective utilization of social science related information by federal policy-makers." Inquiry 13, 3: 239-245.

ROBERTS, A. O. H. and J. K. LARSEN (1971) Effective Use of Mental Health Research Information. AIR 820. Palo Alto, CA: American Institutes for Research.

SMITH, R. L., F. HAWKENSHIRE, and R. O. LIPPITT (1969) Work Orientations of Teenagers. Ann Arbor: Institute for Social Research, University of Michigan.

SOLOFF, ASHER et al. (1975) "Running a research utilization laboratory." Rehabilitation Counseling Bulletin, Special Issue: "Research utilization in rehabilitation." 19, 2: 416-424.

VAN den BAN, ANNE W. (1963) "Utilization and publication of findings," in C. H. Backstrom and G. D. Hursh (eds.) Survey Research Methods in Developing Nations. Chicago: Northwestern University.

VAN de VALL, MARK, CHERYL BOLAS, and TAI S. KANG (1976) "Applied social research in industrial organizations: an evaluation of functions, theory, and methods." Journal of Applied Behavioral Science 12, 2: 158-177.

WEISS, CAROL H. [ed.] (1977) Using Social Research in Public Policy Making. Lexington, MA: D. C. Heath.

WILSON, ELMO C. (1961) "The application of social research findings," pp. 47-58 in Case Studies in Bringing Behavioral Science into Use: Studies in the Utilization of Behavioral Science, Vol. 1. Palo Alto, CA: Institute for Communication Research, Stanford University.

Chapter 6

CONCLUSIONS AND PERSPECTIVES

This concluding chapter has several purposes. First, it will present briefly additional information from the study that is relevant and interesting but somewhat ancillary to what was presented previously. Second, it will summarize some of the main highlights in the overall analysis. Third, it will place the analysis in perspective and suggest further lines of inquiry and action.

ADMINISTRATORS' VIEWS OF RESEARCH

In the course of the interviews, agency directors were requested to indicate their views of the values of research for their work. Specifically, they were asked: "In general, have you found social research information to be of assistance in planning decisions of your department? Please explain." The responses reveal varying outlooks on the part of operational people in administrative posts. Eleven of the twelve executives indicated that research information was of assistance to them. (The remaining executive stated that it was useful "to some degree.") The selection of a sample of relatively successful research utilization sites probably accounts for this response pattern, and the responses could be viewed as a form of validation of the selection procedures.

The views of the executives fell generally into five categories:

Research Aids Planning by Giving Specific Factual Information That Is Useful in Making Decisions

We were able to obtain hard information about the current level of service, including shortfalls. This helps identify need and tells us where to allocate resources.

Several executives cited instances in which factual information had aided in specific, short-term service questions, such as with multiple offender delinquents, meals-on-wheels, and day care for the elderly. Other executives spoke of assistance of factual information in long-range planning, including the setting of long-term priorities.

Research Provides Objectivity in a Complex and Highly Pressured Operational Environment

Because of the many demands on the department, research is useful in enabling one to see the forest, not only the trees.

I start from the view that I can't make decisions without research information. It is essential to me because it is neutral and objective.

We don't have a good knowledge and theory base in the social services field and in the social work profession. Objective information is important when you do not have a firm theory base to operate from. Too many people in the field proceed on the basis of hunches.

Research Is Useful in Correcting False Assumptions and Organizational Myths About the Service Situation

Some studies have overturned broad assumptions of staff that were not accurate. For example, we hired more people to assist in the transport of children. Later we found that little staff time was consumed in transport. Studies have corrected inaccurate impressions that lead to bad delivery of services.

Research Serves as a Weapon in Attaining
Certain Objectives

It can help win resources — In our current situation "knowledge is power." Information from research helps us in the competition for funds from the council. Council members insist on evidence before releasing resources. Our research capability has given us an edge over other departments in this competition.

It can help change attitudes — Research hasn't given me any blinding new insights. But it has helped in educating the staff and committee members. We are dealing with attitudes that are partially political. It is useful to convince people through data rather than trying to deal directly with their feelings.

Research May Have a Cumulative Effect
in Influencing Organizational Decisions

It is the total corpus of research within the department rather than any single study that has an impact on planning.

It is interesting to examine the responses of research staff to a parallel question that asked for their perceptions of the use of research by the director and other managers in the organization. The replies were similar in indicating that all of the administrators found research to be of at least some assistance. There were no "no" responses. However, only seven of the researchers responded with a straight "yes" (in comparison with eleven directors), and five responded "to some degree" (in comparison with one director). Some researchers state that managers are influenced by too many, inappropriate, extraneous factors; acceptance of research is uneven in the organization; and it takes time to gain acceptance of the research function in the organization. On the other hand, several researchers spoke of determined, intelligent, and enlightened use of research by directors. Apparently, some researchers may exaggerate the importance that should be attached to research in the overall organizational scheme of things, whereas some directors may use it in an inadequate or inappropriate way.

In summary, then, this group of executives sees research as useful in:

(1) giving them specific factual information for short-term and long-term planning
(2) correcting false assumptions
(3) providing weapons for resource acquisition and attitude change
(4) building up a cumulative information base in the organization

It can be assumed that research will be used by organization administrators to the degree that it serves such purposes, and to the degree that they come to perceive research produced within the organization in that light. Researchers, therefore, have both *functional* and *interpretive* tasks to deal with in putting the results of their efforts to work.

SOURCES OF RESEARCH INFORMATION

Having examined the perceived usefulness of research to executives, we will now analyze the sources they turn to for such research. Here we will be interested in the scope of sources drawn upon in the search for information. We will also attempt to determine the relative weight they place on their internal research unit, as compared to external information sources.

To get at these issues, the following question was routinely put to each of the administrators in the study:

Do you ever obtain social research information from any of the following sources?
  Books
  Professional and learned journals
  Popular magazines

Newspapers
Television and radio
Reports of your own department's research section
Governmental reports of departments of any kind[1]
Governmental reports prepared by outside researchers
Use of outside consultants
Reports by independent committees, research institutes,
   and so on
Submission by interest groups
Attendance at conferences
Others

Respondents were also asked to indicate in order the three sources they relied upon most frequently for obtaining such information, and to state why they went to those sources most frequently. Researchers were asked a parallel set of questions concerning their perception of the director's use of information sources. The list was based upon the work of Caplan et al. (1975), but was expanded as a result of pretest interviews in the local situation.

The analysis revealed that administrators indicate a wide range of sources for information. The respondents checked a minimum of eight and a maximum of twelve sources, with ten and eleven total choices representing the mode. Administrators in high-utilization organizations such as those in this sample apparently seek multiple sources of information to guide their decision. Their comments in the interviews specifically articulate this:

I can't afford to miss anything.
I must keep my antennae out in all directions.
I'm supposed to do my homework.
One piece of information leads me to another.

Verification for the reports of the directors comes from the research staff, who perceived the range of sources in an almost identical way:

He has wide interests.
He reads a lot.
He uses a huge number of sources.

The least used source was consultants, probably because this is the only one requiring a substantial financial investment to constitute an available input. (The internal research unit also requires financial commitment, but it is a constant and mandatory variable in this situation.)

An arbitrary weighting scheme was used to assess the intensity of reliance placed upon each of the sources. A source that was ranked first by a respondent in frequency of use was given a score of 3; a second rank earned a score of 2; and a third rank, a score of 1. The two top sources in aggregate weighting are indicated below, with an indication of the number of mentions among the twelve directors who were interviewed. Only these top two are listed as they outranked all the others in score by a wide margin:[2]

Source[2]	Weighted Score	Number of times mentioned in first three ranks	Number of first-rank mentions
Own internal section	24	9	7
Government departments	20	10	2

There is a distinct tendency in the direction of the internal research unit and official government reports. The responses on the governmental item also reflect an internal tendency. In most instances mentions are related to the Department of Health and Social Security, which is a national bureau holding considerable authority over local social service departments, authority that is shared to a degree with county or borough levels of government. Some analogy can be made to the relationship between the Department of Health and Human Services and local departments of public welfare, but the degree of direct administrative and financial control in the British situation is a great deal stronger.

The directors see a number of advantageous attributes of internal research units. Among these are:

Provision of Task-Specific Information

Studies represent a consensus by operating division of their information needs. These studies answer the questions that are important to us.

The section studies show trends in my area and relate them to wider national trends.

Gives me concise and practical information about local needs and problems, which aids in departmental program planning.

Timely

The information is up to the minute in relation to our local situation.

Convenient

The section office is just down the hall.

Trustworthy and Personal

The information comes from colleagues with whom I have close working relationships and in whom I have a feeling of confidence.

Integrated Organizational Relationship

These reports are necessary reading because of my general concern and responsibility for departmental matters.

Embracing of Available Information

This source embraces all the other sources of information. I expect the section to cull and summarize whatever information is available that has bearing on our work.

With respect to reports by *governmental departments*, the following reasons were offered for reliance upon them:

Obligatory, Intrusive Aspect

We have a statutory relationship to the national government and are responsible to it.

These become statements of national policy, and you can't afford to ignore them.

They will be pushed down our throats later anyway — that's where the money comes from.

Resource Acquisition

These reports give you an idea of how you will be resourced (and assessed).

There are matters of public finance involved — cuts and priorities affecting local social services.

These reorts offer arguments for influencing council policy. Because this is an authoritative source, it can give you strong arguments.

Provides Social Services-Relevant Information

These reports are geared to local departments — they are related to my work tasks.

Provides Comparative Social Services Information

Tells us what is happening nationally.

Gives us an idea of trends and how we fit in — where we are doing well and where the shortfalls are so we can give those areas more attention and resources.

Expert-Authoritative Aspect

The reports are reliable. We can trust them with regard to complex problems. They are unbiased and informed as well as professionally prepared.

Constitutional Relationship and Responsibility

The director sees his job defined in the statute. We are also substantially funded by DHSS. Therefore, the director feels it is a responsibility of his position to link DHSS with the department and council.

Direct Contact and Expectation

The government sends them to you directly and expects you to read them.

With regard to the less-used sources, some differences were detected between the response of administrators and research staff. Administrators indicated somewhat heavier reliance on *books* and somewhat less reliance on *interest groups* than perceived by the research staff. While researchers thought administrators made very little use of books, administrators themselves offered such comments as:

> Books keep me up to date, even if they are not directly related to departmental work.
>
> I weigh them — glance them over to get a general impression.
>
> Books are authoritative. If a publisher evaluates a manuscript and decides to print it, it must contain something of note.

Books are, apparently, at least scanned by some directors.

The comments by researchers concerning interest groups revealed some measure of disapproval about administrators being influenced by local pressures rather than by objective data. The character of the comments by the two sets of informants shows alternative stances toward interest groups. Administrators commented:

> These groups keep me informed about local concerns and issues.
>
> This information comes from people who are deeply committed and really know the problem.
>
> This is a politically sensitive matter. Council members are responsible to these pressure groups and will be influenced by them, ultimately.

Researchers made these points:

> It's a matter of the director's personality. He likes to deal with community groups and be seen as responsive to them.
>
> The director wants to be seen as supporting the community and doing well by it.

Some researchers acknowledged a need to be responsive to community groups: "These pressure groups lobby actively and have influence. You ignore them at your peril."

Administrators, apparently, portray their involvement with local interest groups as a more genuine and legitimate aspect of information-gathering and agency administration than is perceived by researchers. Researchers see this to a greater degree in the light of personality needs, public relations, and politics. It would seem that interest groups can have both informational and political effects, neither of which should be ignored or overemphasized.

POSSIBLE APPLICATION PRESCRIPTIONS

There are a number of application inferences that grow out of findings on the two most frequently used sources, particularly in examining the reasons they are relied upon. Placing the descriptive information reviewed in the last several pages into active form results in certain implications for researchers:

From the Internal Unit Data

Make the research relevant and task specific to the administrator's basic functions.

Make information timely — current to the operational situation.

Make the information convenient to obtain and use.

Develop a personal relationship — build trust.

Tie the information into the broader administrative running of the organization.

Embrace and synthesize information from a wide range of sources.

From the Governmental Reports Data

Relate the research to certain official or obligatory demands on the user. Explain how it is responsive to such demands.

Have the report intrude into the normal work tasks and routines of the user.

Indicate the potential of the report for increasing resources (when applicable).

Make the report clearly related to the functional domain of the organization (social services, mental health, vocational programming, and so on).

Place the local situation in context — provide comparative information from other situations.

Make the report as authoritative as possible — convey this.

These prescriptions are not all of the same order, and some are easier to operationalize than others. Nevertheless, the results of the interviews suggest that efforts to experiment with them and work them through could have positive outcomes. They suggest strategies that might be employed by researchers external to an organization who wish to influence it and to researchers based within the organization.

ORGANIZATIONAL STYLES OF RESEARCH UTILIZATION

There was no single style or pattern of research utilization activity within the organizations we surveyed. Indeed, the approaches were varied and, in some cases, nondescript. Several rather definite tendencies in style, however, were evidenced among the agencies.

Communication Emphasis

One of the research directors interviewed stressed the importance of communication in his work. A great deal of effort was placed in the writing of well-designed and attractive reports. Various versions were prepared for different audiences. There was a great deal of use of pictures, charts, diagrams, and the like. This director felt that each study undertaken should entail a three-way split in time and resources: one-third should be given over to planning and initiating it, one-third to conducting and analyzing it, and one-third to developing reports and communciations. In his view, the last area generally receives scant attention, and this is where the utilization aspect is most implicated. For this reason, he indicated, little effective utilization takes place. It may be of interest to note that this man had been a journalist during a portion of his career before he became a research specialist.

Participation Emphasis

Another research director accented the participation of operational people in the planning and conducting of research. This held a central place in the allocation of her time and the scheduling of her activities. Much of her energy goes into committee meetings and personal conferences with agency staff throughout the organization. Staff were drawn into involvement in defining problems, interpreting data, framing recommendations, and so forth.

When the interviewer mentioned the communication emphasis discussed above, she discounted it. It is not necessary to rely upon written reports, she held, because the findings and other essential aspects of the research should have been internalized by potential users through involvement in all aspects of the research process. The report, then, has a minor rather than a prominent place in this style of utilization. It simply caps a utilization process that has started much earlier down the line. This researcher had been a psychologist before entering the social services field.

Pragmatic Managerial Orientation

While the previous examples illustrated a journalistic and a psychological style, the example described here features a managerial one. Consistent with the foregoing, the research director in this instance had had business training and had functioned previously in managerial positions. The following elements of the approach were identified by the respondent. Relate studies to immediate pressing problems in the organization. Avoid extensive studies but aim, rather, for a larger number of short-term projects. In these, emphasize feasibility (what is possible) and immediate payoffs (specific benefits to council members, managers, and staff). Work through top and middle management and do not dwell on broad participation. Carefully plan a program of studies on a yearly basis and keep a tight and efficient schedule. The studies should seek to cover the department as a whole, comprehensively, rather than to focus on specific segments or problems of the department. The fiscal and managerial concerns of the department should be prominent in selecting studies, and concerns of practitioner field staff should not weigh too heavily in this. Avoid the more difficult staff and those involved in less definable or measurable activities from a research standpoint. There is more general payoff to the organization in studies that involve more cooperation and malleable staff and those whose activities readily lend themselves to existing research procedures and analytic treatments. A record of successful projects that bring tangible benefits assures continued support from funding sources and leads operational staff to support research follow-through on the results of the studies.

Research in the Middle of the Organization

One administrator had established an arrangement whereby research is joined with planning in a specialized unit' located physically and administratively in "the middle of the organization." It is separate from line managers and from the chief administrator. Field staff are authorized to communicate with the unit without going through their administrative heads. The unit office is situated in the center of the building, just off the main conference rooms where the staff congregate for meetings and informal social contacts. The unit takes responsibility for putting out the departmental newsletter and for arranging social affairs involving the staff. Heavy use is made of development panels composed of cross sections of personnel and staffed by the special unit. These panels "float" within the organization, free of ties or responsibilities to existing department structures. Only after they have had an oppotunity to act on a matter do they engage with the regular organizational machinery. Research is said to gain the support of operational staff because it is close to their center of gravity. It is not situated at the top of the organization where it can be viewed as a tool of management, nor is it in an outside academic institute where it can be viewed as aloof and overly technical.

Research as a "Needling" Force in the Organization

This approach also sets research off and apart from the administrative center of the organization. Not only does research have distance from the executive, but it is somewhat in tension with that position. The research unit in this conception is highly critical, cynical, and innovative. It looks for soft spots, misconceptions, and gaps in the agency situation. A way it does this is through a New Projects Seminar that is composed of a cross section of staff who are willing to take a reflective look at agency problems and to devise solutions free of existing arrangements and assumptions. This seminar group is akin to a "think tank" that functions within the organization but is psychologically detached from it. This approach was developed and described by a research director who also had a planning role within the organization and who had functioned previously as a professional social worker. He was equally interested and qualified in practice as he was in research. The approach appeared to have weak footing, however, and to be unstable in the organization. The director viewed it as subversive of his authority and was likely to block utilization of its outputs.

Planning-Research-Development

This format entails a combined unit that divides into three subunits having specialized but integrated functions: planning, research, and development. The planning subunit is closely associated with the top management team and designs the overall program of the combined unit, keeping it consonant with a general administrative overview. The research unit carries out various studies that grow out of, and are articulated with, the framework of planning. This unit was said to have a reflective and intelligence function in organizational planning. The development subunit is the action arm of the combined unit and works closely with the operational divisions. It systematically organizes first-step initiatives in terms of implementing findings and recommendations that emerge from the research subunit. This may involve pilot testing, preparing necessary forms or budget estimates, training staff for new tasks, operationalizing new program directions, and so on, all in cooperation with personnel in field and service divisions. Development teams and task forces are employed for this purpose. This approach emphasizes a logical progression of roles and functions moving from planning to research to implementation/utilization.

It was not possible in the context of the study to state which of these approaches results in highest utilization rates. Other styles and models would no doubt be identified through examining a larger sample of agencies. It is clear that different styles are associated with different professional outlooks, values, and competencies. While the question of organizational styles of research utilization was not a prime focus of attention in this study, it would seem to be a promising area for further inquiry.

A GENERAL SUMMARY

For organizational actors wishing to improve upon an

agency's performance in research utilization, certain guides and suggestions have emerged from this analysis. In the first place, the notion of linkage of research functions and operational functions offers a useful conceptual and action tool. In applying this, it would be well to consider linkage adjustments across a range of organizational areas: structural arrangements in the organization, processes and procedures that expedite linkage, the climate of attitudes and relationships among operational people and researchers, and the character of research products.

Within each of these four broad areas, certain aspects stand out, based upon the number of times they were brought up in the interviews or the animation with which they were emphasized. These impressions of salient variables need to be verified or discounted in further systematic research studies. Meanwhile, they stand as informed judgments drawn from intensive immersion in the subject. This presentation will vary from the previous checklist format in that it will encapsulate salient points and frame differential actions for researchers and administrators.

Structural Factors

Actions by Researchers	**Actions by Administrators**
Make it an overriding objective to win the support of the top executive and other administrators for research functions.	Demonstrate and communicate strong support for research within the organization.
Define research as clearly serving the planning and service functions of the organization. Dialogue with administrators on the meaning of this stance.	Define research as clearly serving the planning and service functions of the organization. Interpret and dialogue with researchers on this.
Press to establish structural linkage to planners and operational people. Try to have the top research position located at high administrative level within the organization. If	Establish structural linkage between researchers and planning and operational people. Locate the top research position at a high administrative level. If feasible,

feasible, seek to establish a high-level specialized unit having joint research and planning functions.

Press to establish special linking mechanisms such as development agents or development work groups.

Seek to round out competencies in the research staff through inclusion of people who have operational and organizational skills in addition to research capabilities.

Press for a sufficient allocation of time for both researchers and operational people to carry out specific research *utilization* activities.

Be aware of and seek to improve the level of political and economic support in the external environmental system for application undertakings.

establish a high-level specialized unit having joint research and planning functions.

Establish special linking mechanisms such as development agents or development work groups.

Round out the competencies in the research staff through inclusion of people who have operational and organizational skills in addition to research capabilities.

Allow a sufficient allocation of time to both researchers and operational people to carry out specific research *utilization* activities.

Be aware of and seek to improve the level of political and economic support in the external environmental system for application undertakings.

Processes and Procedures

Actions by Researchers

Actively involve operational people in diverse aspects of the research process, including:
   Defining problems and identifying research needs
   Carrying out appropriate research tasks
   Developing conclusions, recommendations, and action plans
   Disseminating and interpreting information
   Engaging in developmental activities which concretize and operationalize action implications

Actions by Administrators

Arrange for active participation of operational people with research staff in diverse aspects of the research process, including:
   Defining problems and identifying research needs
   Carrying out appropriate research tasks
   Developing conclusions, recommendations, and action plans
   Disseminating and interpreting information
   Engaging in developmental activities which concretize and operationalize action implications

Press for and help set up appropriate mixed researcher/user task groups to carry out these functions.

Use time strategically and with parsimony in research-process activities.

Formulate a suitable mix of short-term and middle-range projects in order to respond to different needs and pressures.

Establish appropriate mixed researcher/user task groups to carry out these functions.

Structure the use of time strategically and with parsimony for carrying out research-process activities.

Arrange for a suitable mix of short-term and middle-range projects in order for the organization to be able to respond to different needs and pressures.

Attitudes and Interrelationships

Actions by Researchers

Avoid an air of aloofness in your attitude or behavior.

Be responsive and respectful to operational people.

Take an interest in and become informed about operational tasks.

Be aware of the dynamics of organizational processes.

Reach out to operational people — express interest and support.

Get out into agency activities — including group meetings and information associations.

Actions by Administrators

Create a climate of opinion that is supportive of research and its utilization; be an advocate for research in the organization.

Give moral and substantive support to researchers, recognizing that they are in an isolated position in most organizations.

Pave the way for participation of researchers in agency meetings and events. This entails encouraging researchers to take part and stimulating operational people to make them welcome.

Help researchers to understand key organizational problems and to focus their efforts on them.

Make friends for researchers within the organization.

Keep established researcher/user positive relationships stable by providing for continuity of staff.

Research Reports and Products

Actions by Researchers	Actions by Administrators
Focus reports specifically on given agency problems and concerns.	Take ample time to clarify with researchers the specific agency problems and concerns that particular reports should address.
Suggest concrete action steps implied by the findings.	Assist researchers in deriving appropriate action steps from the findings.
Whenever possible, show how agency resources may be conserved or expanded in the context of recommended actions.	Review with researchers the resource situation of the agency and the resource implications of recommended actions. Look for positive resource implications in terms of conserving or expanding resources.
Give the report an authoritative, objective tone.	Critique drafts or reports with respect to their authoritative and objective character.
In terms of style, keep the report as brief as possible, lay it out attractively, use direct, nontechnical language, and have the report self-contained in coverage of the subject matter.	Help researchers to make their reports comprehensible and responsive to users in the agency. Review drafts with researchers in terms of brevity, attractiveness, simplicity of language, and self-contained coverage of the subject matter.
Be aware of psychological and organizational dynamics. Try not to offend, threaten, or put off potential users.	Assist researchers in analyzing psychological and organizational dynamics involved in a given report. Suggest ways of avoiding offending or threatening potential users.
Write different types of reports suited to different audiences.	Suggest different audiences that might be appropriately singled out to receive different forms of the report, and how these different audiences might be addressed and reached.

While many substantive areas are similar for researchers and managers, there is a slightly different emphasis in action steps, and the two parties may interpret the items in different ways. It should be realized that the actors on opposite ends of the research-to-utilization continuum are not expected to carry out these initiatives in isolation from one another. There is a need for dialogue, exchange, and understanding of mutual roles and contributions. In summarizing her study of the use of evaluation research in federal agencies, Young (1968: 23) makes two points that are important:

(1) Evaluations must be utilization-focused. Planning for utilization must be an integral part of evaluation planning from the beginning.
(2) Criteria for assessing the use-relevance of program evaluation are relative rather than absolute. They are themselves a proper topic for negotiation and agreement between evaluators and decision makers.

The views of researchers and administrators on organizational matters are necessarily at variance in some instances. Researchers, because of their training and commitment, will lean in the direction of validity and completeness of data. Administrators, because of their responsibilities, will be pressed to move pragmatically with whatever data are immediately available to offer illumination on, or justification for, actions. There is a natural and continuing tension in this type of situation. Both parties need to hold to their positions while being able to bend somewhat to the arguments and needs of the other. Some midpoint of resolution has to be arrived at again and again through the interplay of perspectives. The above summary guide list should be read in that light.

A FINAL WORD

Litwak and Meyer (1974: vii-viii), with whom the writer

has enjoyed a long and fruitful collegial relationship, concluded their excellent study of school-community relations by
stating: "We hope the results will be posing of significant
hypotheses to be tried by practice and tested by research."
The same type of research-application perspective is pertinent here. Results of the interviews suggest a number of
avenues for further research and for possible guidelines for
organizations desiring to enhance their research utilization
potentialities. It is our hope that this small presentation will
prompt the exploration of these avenues.

From a research standpoint, much additional work is
necessary. One might, for example, compare organizations
designated as high research utilizers with those that are low
utilizers in order to determine whether the variables delineated
here are good discriminators between the two. Can these differences be demonstrated through statistical tests of
significance? Can a ranked hierarchy of importance of
significance among the variables be demonstrated? More
behavioral methods for studying research utilization might be
employed. Observation of specific utilization behavior within
organizations might be attempted, or actual programs carried
out by organizations might be traced back to determine
whether research inputs were involved in their design.

While awaiting more firm knowledge, organizations are
faced with the immediate problem of making their research
products more effectual. The factors that have been brought
forward from the field interviews offer possible guidelines for
organizations seriously concerned with enhancing research
utilization. The state of the literature in this field is such that
few problems have been investigated to the point that
definitive intelligence is at hand. At the same time, the state
of what might be termed "research utilization policy and
practices" is such that guidance needs to be secured from
whatever promising sources are available.

Thus, the hypotheses offered may also be viewed as a set of
tentative prescriptive formulations, to be considered by an

organization seeking to increase its research-utilization capabilities. In such direct application it is necessary to be clear that these are not scientifically tested principles but action ideas that need to be weighted and assessed in a given agency situation by those having experience and judgment within that situation. They constitute an aid to judgment, which is the main basis of practical choice now, and which can serve, in a checklist fashion, to enrich whatever information base is drawn upon in decision-making. Other research evidence that is available and bears on the matter can augment such judgments. Such testing in practice may not only increase the programmatic impact of research utilization, but can feed back on the knowledge base by generating new, interesting, and refined hypotheses. This kind of intimate interplay between action and research is intrinsic in the very concept of research utilization.

"The capacity for acquiring knowledge," said Dr Johnson, "is what distinguishes a man from a beast. The capacity for using that knowledge is what distinguishes a man from a fool."

NOTES

1. This item and the one that follows were collapsed in the analysis.

2. No other source had a weighted score of more than 6, more than one first-rank mention, or more than four total mentions. The perception of research staff about directors' prime sources was strikingly congruent with the directors' self-reports.

REFERENCES

CAPLAN, NATHAN, A. MORRISON and R. STAMBAUGH (1975) The Use of Social Science Knowledge in Policy Decisions at the National Level: A Report to Respondents. Ann Arbor: Institute for Social Research, University of Michigan.
LITWAK, EUGENE and HENRY J. MEYER (1974) School, Family and Neighborhood: The Theory and Practice of School-Community Relations. New York: Columbia University Press.
YOUNG, CARLOTTA J. (1978) "Evaluation Utilization." Presented at Evaluation Research Society Second Annual Meeting, Washington, DC, November.

BIBLIOGRAPHY

ABRAMS, MARK (1974) "Social surveys, social theory and social policy." SSRC Newsletter 24, July: 11-14.

AGARWALA-ROGERS, REHKA (1977) "Why is evaluation research not utilized?" in Marcia Guttentag (ed.) Evaluation Studies Review Annual, Vol. 2. Beverly Hills, CA: Sage.

BECKHARD, RICHARD (1974) "ABS in health care systems: who needs it?" Journal of Applied Behavioral Science 10: 43-106.

BENJAMIN, BERNARD (1972) "Research strategies in social service departments of local authorities in Great Britain." Journal of Social Policy 2, 1: 13-26.

BLUM, R. H. and J. J. DOWNING (1964) "Staff responses to innovation in a mental health service," American Journal of Public Health 54: 1230-1240.

BRIGHT, J. R. (1964) Research, Development, and Technological Innovation: An Introduction. Homewood, IL: Irwin.

BROWN, TIMOTHY (1976) "Guidelines for integrating program evaluation with administrative decision making." Presented at APA Convention, Washington, DC.

CAPLAN, NATHAN (1977) "A minimal set of conditions necessary for the utilization of social science knowledge in policy formulation at the national level," pp. 183-197 in Carol H. Weiss (ed.) Using Social Research in Public Policy Making. Lexington, MA: D. C. Heath.

——— A. MORRISON and R. STAMBAUGH (1975) The Use of Social Science Knowledge in Policy Decisions at the National Level: A Report to Respondents. Ann Arbor: Institute for Social Research, University of Michigan.

CARTER, LAUNOR F. (1968) "Knowledge production and utilization in contemporary organizations," pp. 1-20 in T. L. Eidell and J. M. Kitchel (eds.) Knowledge Production and Utilization in Educational Administration. Eugene: Center for the Advanced Study of Educational Administration, University of Oregon.

CHERNS, ALBERT B. (1970) "Relations between research institutions and users of research." International Social Science Journal 22, 2: 226-242.

——— (1968) "The use of the social sciences." Human Relations 21: 313-325.

CHESLER, MARK and M. FLANDERS (1967) "Resistance to research and research utilization: the death and life of a feedback attempt." Journal of Applied Behavioral Science 3: 467-487.

CHESLER, M. and R. FOX (1967) "Teacher peer relations and educational change." National Educational Association Journal 56, 5: 25-26.

CHURCHMAN, C. WEST (1964) "Managerial acceptance of scientific recommendations." California Management Review 7, 1: 31-38.

COLEMAN, J. S., E. KATZ and H. MENZEL (1966) Medical Innovation: A Diffusion Study. Indianapolis: Bobbs-Merrill.

COOPER, C. R. and B. ARCHAMBAULT [eds.] (1968) Communication,

Dissemination, and Utilization of Research Information in Rehabilitation Counseling. Proceedings of a regional conference sponsored by the Department of Guidance and Psychological Services. Springfield, MA: Springfield College (in collaboration with Rehabilitation Service Administration, Department of Health, Education, and Welfare).

CRAIG, DOROTHY (1975) "A hip pocket guide to planning and evaluation." Mental Health Skills Lab, School of Social Work, University of Michigan, Ann Arbor.

CRANE, D. (1970) "The nature of scientific communication and influence." International Social Science Journal 1: 28-41.

DAVIS, HOWARD and SUSAN SALASIN (1975) "The utilization of evaluation," pp. 621-666 in Elmer Struening and Marcia Guttentag (eds.) Handbook of Evaluation Research, Vol. I, Beverly Hills, CA: Sage.

DONNISON, DAVID (1972) "Research for policy." Minerva 10, 4: 519-536.

EASH, M. J. (1968) "Bringing research findings into classroom practice." Elementary School Journal 68, 8: 410-418.

FLANAGAN, JOHN C. (1961) "Case studies on the utilization of behavioral science research," pp. 36-46 in Case Studies in Bringing Behavioral Science into Use. Studies in the Utilization of Behavioral Science, Vol. 1. Palo Alto, CA: Institute for Communication Research, Stanford University.

GARVEY, W. D. and B. C. GRIFFITH (1967) "Communication in a science: the system and its modification," pp. 16-36 in A. de Reuck and J. Knight (eds.) Communication in Science: Documentation and Automation. A Ciba Foundation Volume. Boston: Little, Brown.

GLASER, EDWARD M. (1973) "Knowledge transfer and institutional change." Professional Psychology 4: 434-444.

——— and C. G. WRENN (1966) Putting Research, Experimental, and Demonstration Findings to Use. Washington, DC: Office of Manpower Policy, Evaluation and Resarch, US Department of Labor.

GLASER, EDWARD M., H. S. COFFEY, J. B. MARKS, and I. B. SARASON (1967) Utilization of Applicable Research and Demonstration Results. Los Angeles: Human Interaction Research Institute.

GLASER, EDWARD M. and S. TAYLOR (1969) Factors Influencing the Success of Applied Research. Washington, DC: National Institute of Mental Health, Department of Health, Education, and Welfare.

GLASER, EDWARD M. and T. E. BACKER (1975) "Evaluating the research utilization specialist." Rehabilitation Counseling Bulletin 19, 2: 387-395.

GLAZER, BARNEY G. and ANSELM L. STRAUSS (1967) The Discovery of Grounded Theory. Chicago: Aldine.

GLOCK, CHARLES Y. (1961) "Applied social research: some conditions affecting its utilization," pp. 1-19 in Case Studies in Bringing Behavioral Science into Use: Studies in the Utilization of Behavioral Science, Vol. 1. Palo Alto, CA: Institute for Communication Research, Stanford University.

GOLDSTEIN, MICHAEL S., ALFRED C. MARCUS, and NANCY P. RAUSCH (1978) "The nonutilization of evaluation research." Pacific Sociological Review 21, 1: 21-44.

GUBA, EGON, G. (1975) "Problems in utilizing the results of evaluation." Journal of Research and Development in Education 8, 3: 42-54.

——— (1968) "Development, diffusion and evaluation," pp. 37-63 in T. L. Eidell and J. M. Kitchel (eds.) Knowledge Production and Utilization in Educational Administration. Eugene: Center for the Advanced Study of Educational Administration, University of Oregon.

GUETZKOW, HAROLD (1959) "Conversion barriers in using the social sciences." Administrative Science Quarterly 4: 68-81.

GUREL, LEE (1975) "The human side of evaluating human services programs," pp. 11-28 in Marcia Guttentag and Elmer Struening (eds.) Handbook of Evaluation Research, Vol. 2. Beverly Hills, CA: Sage.

HALPERT, HAROLD P. (1966) "Communication as a basic tool in promoting utilization of research findings." Community Mental Health Journal 2, 3: 231-236.

HAVELOCK, RONALD G. (1968) "Dissemination and translation roles," pp. 64-119 in T. L. Eidell and J. M. Kitchel (eds.) Knowledge Production and Utilization in Educational Administration. Eugene: Center for the Advanced Study of Educational Administration, University of Oregon.

——— (1968) "New developments in translating theory and research into practice." Presented at the 96th Annual Meeting of the American Public Health Association, Detroit, November.

——— (1969) Planning for Innovation Through Dissemination and Utilization of Knowledge. Ann Arbor: Center for Research on Utilization of Scientific Knowledge, Institute for Social Research, University of Michigan.

——— (1969) "Translating theory into practice." Rehabilitation Record (November-December): 24-27.

——— and DAVID A. LINGWOOD (1973) R & D Utilization Strategies and Functions: An Analytical Comparison of Four Systems. Ann Arbor: Institute for Social Research, University of Michigan.

HAVELOCK, RONALD G. and E. A. MARKOWITZ (1973) Highway Safety Research Communication: Is There a System? Ann Arbor: Institute for Social Research, University of Michigan.

JOLY, JEAN-MARIE (1967) "Research and innovation: two solitudes?" Canadian Education and Research Digest 2: 184-194.

JUNG, CARL and RONALD LIPPITT (1966) "The study of change as a concept in research utilization." Theory into Practice 2, 1: 25-29.

KLEIN, HELEN D. (1968) "The Missouri story: a chronicle of research utilization and program planning." Presented at the National Conference of Social Welfare.

KNEZO, GENEVIEVE J. (1974) Program Evaluation: Emerging Issues of Possible Legislative Concern Relating to the Conduct and Use of Evaluation in the Congress and the Executive Branch. Washington, DC: Congressional Research Service.

KOGAN, L. S. (1963) "The utilization of social work research." Social Casework 44: 569-574.

LIKERT, RENSIS and RONALD LIPPITT (1963) "The utilization of social science," in L. Festinger and D. Katz (eds.) Research Methods in the Behavioral Sciences. New York: Dryden.

LIPPITT, RONALD and RONALD HAVELOCK (1968) "Needed research on research utilization," in Research Implication for Educational Diffusion. East Lansing: Department of Education, Michigan State University.

LITWAK, EUGENE and HENRY J. MEYER (1974) School, Family and Neighborhood: The Theory and Practice of School-Community Relations. New York: Columbia University Press.

LUNDBERG, CRAIG C. (1966) "Middlemen in science utilization: some notes toward clarifying conversion roles." American Behavioral Scientist 9 (February): 11-14.

McCLELLAND, W. A. (1968) "The process of effecting change." Presidential Address to the Division of Military Psychology, American Psychological Association.

MACKIE, R. R. and P. R. CHRISTENSEN (1967) Translation and Application of Psychological Research. Technical Report 716-1. Goleta, CA: Santa Barbara Research Park, Human Factors Research.

MAGISOS, J. H. (1971) Interpretation of Target Audience Needs in the Design of Information Dissemination Systems for Vocational-Technical Education. Columbus: The Center for Vocational and Technical Education, Ohio State University.

MERCER, J. R., H. F. DINGMAN, and G. TARJAN (1964) "Involvement, feedback, and mutuality: principles for conducting mental health research in the community." American Journal of Psychiatry 121, 3: 228-237.

MORIARTY, EDWARD J. (1967) "Summary of small group recommendations," pp. 72-73 in Communication, Dissemination, and Utilization of Rehabilitation Research Information. Studies in Rehabilitation Counselor Training No. 5. Washington, DC: Joint Liaison Committee of the Council of State Administrators of Vocational Rehabilitation and Rehabilitation Counselor Educators, Department of Health, Education, and Welfare.

National Science Foundation (1969) Knowledge into Action: Improving the Nation's Use of the Social Sciences. Report of the Special Commission of the National Science Board. Washington, DC: National Science Foundation.

PAISLEY, WILLIAM J. (1969) "Perspectives on the utilization of knowledge." Presented at the meeting of the American Educational Research Association, Los Angeles. February.

——— (1968) "Information needs and uses," pp. 1-30 in C. A. Cuadra (ed.) Annual Review of Information Science and Technology, Vol. 3. New York: Interscience.

PARKER, E. B. and W. J. PAISLEY (1966) "Research for psychologists on the interface of the scientist and his information system." American Psychologist 21: 1060-1071.

PATTON, MICHAEL Q. et al. (1977) "In search of impact: an analysis of the utilization of federal health evaluation research," pp. 141-163 in Carol H. Weiss (ed.) Using Social Research in Public Policy Making. Lexington, MA: D. C. Heath.

PELLEGRIN, ROLAND J. (1965) "The place of research in planned change," pp. 65-75 in R. O. Carlson et al. Change Processes in the Public Schools. Eugene: Center for the Advanced Study of Educational Administration, University of Oregon.

PELZ, DONALD C. and FRANK M. ANDREWS (1976) Scientists in Organizations: Productive Climates for Research and Development. Ann Arbor: Institute for Social Research, University of Michigan.

POSER, E. G., I. DUNN, and R. M. SMITH (1964) "Resolving conflicts between clinical and research teams." Mental Hospitals 15, 5: 278-282.

RICH, ROBERT F. (1975) "Selective utilization of social science related information by federal policy-makers." Inquiry 13, 3: 239-245.

ROBERTS, A. O. H. and J. K. LARSEN 61971) Effective Use of Mental Health Research Information. AIR 820. Palo Alto, CA: American Institutes for Research.

ROGERS, EVERETT M. (1967) "Communication of vocational rehabilitation innovations," pp. 19-32 in Communication, Dissemination and Utilization of Rehabilitation Research Information. Studies in Rehabilitation Counselor Training, No. 5. Washington, DC: Joint Liaison Committee of the Council of State Administrators of Vocational Rehabilitation and the Rehabilitation Counselor Educators, Department of Health, Education, and Welfare.

――― and F. F. SHOEMAKER (1971) Communication of Innovations: A Cross-Cultural Approach. New York: Macmillan.

ROSE, RICHARD (1977) "Disciplined research and undisciplined problems," pp. 23-35 in Carol H. Weiss (ed.) Using Social Research in Public Policy Making. Lexington, MA: D. C. Heath.

ROSENBLATT, AARON (1968) "The practitioner's use and evaluation of research." Social Work 13: 53-59.

ROSSMAN, BETTY, DIANE HOBER, and JAMES CIARLO (n.d.) "Awareness, use, and consequences of evaluation data in a community mental health center." Unpublished paper, University of Denver.

ROTHMAN, JACK (1974) Planning and Organizing for Social Change: Action Principles from Social Science Research. New York: Columbia University Press.

SCANLON, JOHN and JOHN WALLER (1978) "Program evaluation and better federal programs." Presented at ASPA Conference, Phoenix.

SCHMUCK, RICHARD (1968) "Social psychological factors in knowledge utilization," pp. 143-173 in T. L. Eidell and J. M. Kitchel (eds.) Knowledge Production and Utilization in Educational Administration. Eugene: Center for the Advanced Study of Educational Administration, University of Oregon.

SCHWARTZ, DAVID C. (1966) "On the growing popularization of social science: the expanding public and problems of social science utilization." American Behavioral Scientist 9, 10: 47-50.

SHARPE, L. J. (1975) "The social scientist and policy-making: some cautionary thoughts and transatlantic reflections." Journal of Policy and Politics 4, 2: 7-34.

SHARTLE, CARROLL L. (1961) "The occupational research program: an example of research utilization," pp. 59-72 in Case Studies in Bringing Behavioral Science into Use: Studies in the Utilization of Behavioral Science, Vol. 1. Palo Alto, CA: Institute for Communication Research, Stanford University.

SHORT, E. C. (1973) "Knowledge production and utilization in curriculum: a special case of the general phenomenon." Review of Educational Research 43: 237-301.

SIEBER, S. D., K. S. LOUIS, and L. METZGER (1974) "The use of educational knowledge: evaluation of the pilot state dissemination program," in H. Hug (ed.) Evolution/Revolution: Library-Media-Information Futures. New York: Bowker.

SMITH, GILBERT (1972) "Research policy: 'pure' and 'applied'." British Journal and Social Science Review (April): 723-724.

SMITH, R. L., F. HAWKENSHIRE, and R. O. LIPPITT (1969) Work Orientations of Teenagers. Ann Arbor: Institute for Social Research, University of Michigan.

SOLOFF, ASHER et al. (1975) "Running a research utilization laboratory." Rehabilitation Counseling Bulletin, Special Issue: "Research utilization in rehabilitation." 19, 2: 416-424.

SWANSON, DON R. (1966) "On improving communications among scientists." Bulletin of the Atomic Scientists 22, 2: 8-12.

TROPMAN, PETER J. (1978) "Evaluation, policy making and budgeting: starting from scratch in Wisconsin." Delivered at the National Conference on the Future of Social Work Research, sponsored by the National Association of Social Workers, San Antonio, October.

TWAIN, DAVID, ELEANOR HARLOW, and DONALD MERWIN (1974) Research and Human Services: A Guide to Collaboration for Program Development. Washington, DC: National Institute for Mental Health, Department of Health, Education, and Welfare.

Unco Inc. (1973) Communication Model for the Utilization of Technical Research (CMUTR) Study: Utilization of Advanced Management Innovations Within State Departments of Public Welfare. Washington, DC: Author.

U.S. Department of Health, Education, and Welfare (1963) Research Utilization in Aging: An Exploration. Washington, DC: Government Printing Office.

VAN den BAN, ANNE W. (1963) "Utilization and publication of findings," in C. H. Backstrom and G. D. Hursh (eds.) Survey Research Methods in Developing Nations., Chicago: Northwestern University Press.

VAN de VALL, MARK, CHERYL BOLAS, and TAI S. KANG (1976) "Applied social research in industrial organizations: an evaluation of functions, theory, and methods." Journal of Applied Behavioral Science 12, 2: 158-177.

WEISS, CAROL H. (1977) "Methods for studying the usefulness of sociological research." Presented at 72nd Annual Meeting of American Sociological Association, Chicago.

——— (1977) "What makes social research usable: data from mental health." Prepared for annual meeting of the American Association for the Advancement of Science, Denver, February.

——— [ed.] (1977) Using Social Research in Public Policy Making. Lexington, MA: D. C. Heath.

WILSON, ELMO C. (1961) "The application of social research findings," pp. 47-58 in Case Studies in Bringing Behavioral Science Into Use: Studies in the Utilization of Behavioral Science, Vol. 1. Palo Alto, CA: Institute for Communication Resarch, Stanford University.

WILSON, JAMES Q. (1978) "Social science and public policy: a personal note," in Laurence E. Lynn, Jr. (ed.) Knowledge and Policy: The Uncertain Connection. Washington, D. C.: National Academy of Sciences.

WOLFENSBERGER, WOLF (1969) "Dilemmas of research in human management agencies." Rehabilitation Literature (June): 162-169.

YOUNG, CARLOTTA J. (1978) "Evaluation utilization." Presented at Evaluation Research Society Second Annual Meeting, Washington, DC, November.

APPENDIX A
INTERVIEW GUIDE FORM

USE OF SOCIAL RESEARCH INFORMATION IN LOCAL AUTHORITY SOCIAL SERVICES PLANNING

The study focuses on use of social research information in planning decisions. In particular, it will concentrate on those instances where research information has been successfully applied. Through this approach, it is the intention of the study to suggest ways by which existing research information may more likely and effectively be brought to bear on the planning process.

Interviews are being conducted in some 12 local departments in and around London. Both the director and the senior research person are being interviewed.

All information given in the interview will be treated in a confidential and sensitive manner. Any written reports will emphasize generalisations concerning optimizing research utilization. Specific names of authorities or participants will not be related to findings, except when approval is specifically given. Attention is being given to procedures for rapid feedback of findings to participants and interested professionals.

The study is an adapted replication of one conducted by The Institute of Social Research, University of Michigan, in Washington, DC.

For purposes of the interview, social research information is defined as follows:

The term social research information is used broadly in this study. It implies 'findings' or 'data' obtained from various sources in various ways. This may range from theoretical studies conducted by social scientists in academic institutions to statistical analyses of service records carried out by research staff in local social service departments. Social research as used here means empirically based factual information concerning social phenomena — behaviour, processes, structures (population characteristics, attitudes, services, patterns, outcomes, etc).

USE OF SOCIAL RESEARCH INFORMATION
IN LOCAL AUTHORITY SOCIAL SERVICES PLANNING

Senior Research Officer's Questionnaire

Date _____

1   Local authority   2 Person
     department _____   Interviewed _____

3   Title of your position _____

   A   How would you define your main job functions?
       _____
       _____
       _____

   B   How many professional researchers are there in the
       research section?
       _____

   C   Is there a senior planning group or directorate in the
       department?
                    YES _____NO _____
   D   If yes, please describe the composition of the group
       _____
       _____

   E   What is your relationship to the director or the senior plan-
       ning group?
       _____
       _____

   F   Do you have an organizational chart that I can take with
       me?
       _____

4 In general, is social research information seen by the director (and other senior managers) to be of assistance in making departmental planning decisions?

    YES ☐   NO ☐   TO SOME DEGREE ☐

Please explain:

_____

_____

5 Does the director ever obtain social research information from any of the following sources (tick ( ) all that apply)

(a) ☐ Books

(b) ☐ Professional and learned journals

(c) ☐ Popular magazines

(d) ☐ Newspapers

(e) ☐ Television and radio

(f) ☐ Reports of his own local departmental research section

(g) ☐ Government reports of departments of any kind

(h) ☐ Reports prepared for government by outside consultants

(i) ☐ Use of outside consultants

(j) ☐ Reports of independent committees, research institutes, etc

(k) ☐ Submission of interest groups

(l) ☐ Attendance at conferences, seminars, etc

(m) ☐ Other (please specify)

_____

6 Which three are the most relied upon by him for obtaining such information, and what accounts for their more frequent use?

	Source	why used
Most frequent	_____	_____
Second most frequent	_____	_____
Third most frequent	_____	_____

7 Are you or other research staff used to help seek pertinent research information from various existing sources?

Yes ☐   Occasionally ☐   Regularly ☐

No ☐

(a) In what way(s):

_____

_____

_____

Staff name   Title

_____   _____
_____   _____

8   What accounts for being used in this way?
    _____
    _____
    _____

9   Can you recall an instance when a specific study or report was
    used by the director (or other senior managers) as the basis for
    the planning decision?

    (a) YES   (b) NO   TURN to No 24

10 Would you briefly describe the general circumstances surroun-
    ding this decision. I will ask you a series of more specific ques-
    tions in just a moment
    _____
    _____
    _____
    _____
    _____
    _____
    _____

11 Did the problem appear first and lead to seeking pertinent
    research information ☐ or was research information available
    first and applied to an existing problem ☐
    Explain:
    _____
    _____
    _____
    _____

12 The specific decision or problem _____
    _____

13 The specific study or report (author, title, reference, etc., or a
    brief description) (is *a copy available* for me to have?)
    _____
    _____

14 The form(s) of the study or report that was used (book, departmental research report, journal article, news account, staff summary, staff memo, etc) was the research information reported in multiple forms? (please specify)

_____

_____

15 Method used in the study (demographic data, program evaluation, opinion survey, etc)

_____

_____

16 How definite/tentative were the findings or conclusions of the study?

_____

_____

17 Were practical applications specified?

_____

_____

18 Initiation:
   ☐ Did the director (or senior manager(s) locate or indicate the study? Indicate circumstances

   _____

   _____

   ☐ Or was it passed on to them? _____

   _____

   By what procedure or manner passed on? _____

   _____

19 What about the study or report made it seem relevant and useful in this situation?
   (a) aspects of the study itself (subject, form, sponsorship, author, method of presentation, etc)

   _____

   _____

   _____

   (b) aspects of the situation or circumstances prevailing at that time

   _____

   _____

   _____

20 Were there any specific activities you or other research staff engaged in relative to the study that helped facilitate its use?

_____

_____

21 Were there any specific activities that the director or managers engaged in relative to the study that helped facilitate its use?

_____

_____

22 At what stage in the development of the decision was the study introduced?

_____

_____

_____

23 In what ways was the study actually used (current status)?

_____

_____

_____

24 Can you recall an instance when social research information was specifically ignored or rejected by senior managers in making a planning decision?

    (a) YES   (b) NO   TURN to No 26

25 The specific decision and circumstances _____

_____

26 The specific study or report _____

_____

_____

27 Why was the study: ignored ☐   or rejected ☐ :
    (a) Aspects of the study itself _____

         _____

         _____

         _____

         _____

         _____

(b) Aspects of the situation _____

_____

_____

_____

_____

_____

_____

28 Do you feel there are factors that work in favour of or against the use of social research information within your organization?

| (a) YES
work for | (b) YES
work
against | (c) NO TURN
to No 29 |

What are the factors that work for the use of such information?

What are the factors that work against the use of such information?

Organizational factors

Organizational factors

Other factors

Other factors

These are some summary questions in this section about problems of using social research information, and about relationships between social service directors-managers and researchers.

29(a) What would you say are the main problems you encounter in having social research information used (reports, data) for planning?

_____

_____

_____

_____

29(b) What specific suggestions do you have concerning how such information might become more useful/used in planning?

_____

_____

_____

_____

30(a) What would you say are some of the main problems pertaining to relationships between directors (and other managers) and researchers in local authority social service departments?

_____

_____

_____

_____

30(b) What suggestions do you have for improving working relationships between directors (and other managers) and research staff:

First, suggestions for directors and managers _____

_____

_____

Now, suggestions for researchers _____

_____

_____

SECTION B: BACKGROUND INFORMATION

There are a few concluding questions about your background and the interview will be finished. (Please fill out this section yourself).

B1   What is the date of your birth? _____ _____

(month)   (year)

B2 Would you tell me about your educational background?
Higher Education

Institution attended	*Degree*	*Specialization*

B3 To what degree would you say that you engaged in studies in the social sciences (sociology, political science, anthropology, psychology) while you were a student?

1 MUCH   2 SOME   3 LITTLE   4 NONE

B3(a) How long have you been employed professionally in a social research capacity?

_____   _____
(years)   (months)

B4 Are you a qualified social worker?
YES ☐
NO   ☐

B5 How long have you worked in social services/social work field?

_____   _____
(years)   (months)

B6 In this social services department?

_____   _____
(years)   (months)

B7 How long have you held your present position?

_____   _____
(years)   (months)

THANK YOU FOR YOUR ASSISTANCE

APPENDIX B

ILLUSTRATIVE DOCUMENTS
FROM FIELD AGENCIES

B1

**ILLUSTRATIVE STUDY REPORT
FROM A FIELD AGENCY
(with Emphasis on Communication to the Reader)**

A REPORT ON

*The reasons for admitting
children to day nurseries*

Summary of Findings

(1) The unsupported lone parent not coping adequately with the child's upbringing constituted over half of all the reasons given for admitting the children presently either attending the Council's day nurseries or being paid for at private nurseries (para. 3.11).

(2) Medical problems relating to either a parent or the child accounted for nearly one-third of the reasons (para. 3.11).

(3) Low standard of child care accounted for about one-sixth of all reasons (para. 3.11).

(4) There were also a few cases where the day nursery place was being used to prevent a child being received into care (Attachment II).

(5) It is believed that these reasons for admission reasonably reflect the incidence and strength of problems in the community (para. 3.14).

(6) There are differences in the breakdown of reasons between the five Social Work Areas which the social work staff might wish to speculate on (para. 3.7).

Background

1.1 The Corporate Planning Unit and the Social Services Research and Planning Section have been carrying out a study* ("The Priority Areas for Day Nurseries"; Joint Report to be published shortly) which aims to give advice on the siting of new day nurseries.

1.2 In the course of that study, an index to reflect the relative need for day nursery places in different parts of the borough was constructed.

1.3 Such an index has to be based on an understanding of the needs that day nurseries are designed to meet and consequently the Research and Planning Section studies the reasons which led to the admission of children currently attending day nurseries. The results have been incorporated into the day nursery location study.

Method

2.1 During June 1975, the under-5 specialist in each Area was asked to record, for each child attending a day nursery on her files, the appropriate reason or reasons for admission. Where the circumstances had changed since a child had been originally admitted, the social worker was asked to record the current reason or reasons for the child being retained in the nursery.

2.2 The following is a full list of the reasons given by the social workers during the study:

(a) unsupported, lone parent who is not coping adequately with the child's upbringing

(b) medical reasons relating to a parent

(c) medical reasons relating to the child

(d) to allow a child to be removed from 'in care'

(e) low standard of child care — poor home conditions leading to lack of stimulation

(f) low standard of child care — risk of neglect leading to risk of physical injury

(g) low standard of child care — potential battered baby at risk of physical assault

2.3 Where there was more than one reason mentioned in the file, the social worker was asked to rank the reasons in order of importance but to include only reasons that alone would have been sufficient to justify admission to a day nursery. The fact that children were members of the same family was not taken into account.

Results

3.1 There are three main ways of analysing the results of a study such as this where the number of reasons per child varied:

(a) breakdown of the sole reasons for admission, i.e., those cases where only one reason was given

(b) breakdown of the principal reasons for admission, i.e., the sole reason where only one reason was given together with the first reason where more than one reason was given

(b) breakdown of all reasons for admission

3.2 This report gives the above three analyses in full in Attachment I, and the total number of items that each reason occurred at each individual day nursery is given in Attachment II.

3.3 In the body of the Report, however, comment is confined to the principal reasons, i.e., the results of the survey were studied as if the social workers had been allowed to put down only one reason for admitting each child. Although "all reasons" gives a more complete picture of the incidence of problems amongst the children, "principal reason" was selected as a more reliable basis for discussing the results of the survey because it was felt that it must have been very difficult for social workers to judge the urgency of secondary reasons for admitting children. Some secondary reasons may therefore have been included which would not, by themselves, have been sufficiently urgent to have justified admitting the child.

3.4 The data cover 409 children out of a possible total of 468 children. These were made up of 358 out of 370 children on the register of Council day nurseries at the time of the study and 51 out of 98 children supported by the Council in private day nurseries or in nurseries belonging to other local authorities (A and C Areas only).

3.5 For various reasons the files of the remaining children were unavailable at the time of the interviews. However, a sample of 409 out of a total of 468 children can reasonably be expected to be representative and this was used, in order not to delay the study.

3.6 The number of children recorded in each social work area was as follows:

S.W. Area	Number of children	%
B	99	24
E	93	23
A	85	21
D	69	17
C	63	15
Total	409	100

3.7 There are some differences in the breakdown of principal reasons for admission between the five social work Areas which are just statistically significant. Figure 1 below shows the variations.

FIG. 1   Analysis of Principal Reasons for Admission in Each Social Work Area

Percentage of times 'unsupported parent' was given as a principal reason.

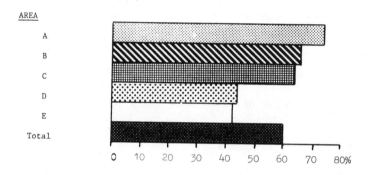

Percentage of times 'medical problem' was given as a principal reason.

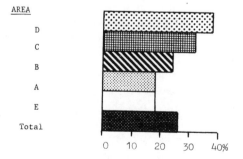

The remaining reasons occurred so infrequently that they cannot be shown in this way. They will be found in the Attachments.

3.8 It may be of interest to social work staff to speculate on possible explanations of why, for example, in A "unsupported parent" is a relatively strong reason and "medical problem" a weak reason, whilst in D the reverse is the case.

3.9 However, too much should not be read into these differences since the results of this study give us only a snapshot of the position at a certain time. The normal turnover of children would be expected to change the pattern of reasons in each Area from time to time.

3.10 Hence it seems reasonable to amalgamate the results from the five Areas and this has been done in Table 1 and Chart 1 in Attachment I for all reasons.

3.11 The principal reasons can be grouped together into four types, the percentage occurrence of which is, as follows:

Type of reason	Percentage Occurrence
Unsupported parent	58
Medical problems	24
Low standard of child care	17
Removal from "in care"	1

3.12 These results show that unsupported lone parent is the dominant reason for admission, and that medical problems and low standard of child care are not insignificant.

3.13 The day nursery location study is concerned with the siting of additional nurseries. It is therefore relevant to ask how far the reasons for admission of the children at present attending day nurseries reflect the incidence of problems amongst those who have applied for places, at least over the period of time that these admissions took place?

3.14 Whilst it is impossible to give a firm answer to this question, the truth is probably that the reasons for admission reasonably reflect the incidence of problems. Over the period of time that the children at present atending day nurseries were admitted, there has always been a much greater demand for places than there have been vacancies. Thus social workers have always been in the position of having to select children for admission from a large number of bona fide applicants. The children who were chosen can therefore be thought of as being a sample of those who applied and we can assume that the reasons given in this study approximately reflect the incidence and urgency of problems amongst those who applied for places. This would be grossly untrue only if all applicants in one or more categories of children had been provided with a place; there is no suggestion that any such saturation point has ever been reached.

Attachment I to Appendix B1

ATTACHMENT I(a): Analysis of Reasons for Admission When Only One, Sole Reason Was Given

Sole reason	Number of children in:						
	Area B	Area D	Area A	Area C	Area E	Total	% in LBW
Unsupported parent	58	27	50	38	30	203	67
Medical (parent)	11	9	2	7	1	30	10
Medical (child)	11	7	4	4	14	40	13
Removal from "in care"	1	1	0	0	0	2	1
Poor home conditions	2	0	2	2	0	6	2
Risk of neglect	1	2	0	1	4	8	3
Potential battered baby	2	6	2	0	3	13	4
Total number of children for whom only one reason was given	86	52	60	52	52	302	100

NOTE: For interest, it should be noted that:

    302 children were admitted for 1 reason
     95   2 reasons
     10   3 reasons
      2   4 reasons
    409 total children

ATTACHMENT I(b): Analysis of the Principal Reasons for Admission

Principal reason	Number of times each reason was given as a principal reason in:					Total	% in LBW
	Area B	Area D	Area A	Area C	Area E		
Unsupported parent	65	30	61	40	38	234	58
Medical (parent)	11	14	5	11	3	44	10
Medical (child)	13	12	10	9	14	58	14
Removal from "in care"	1	1	0	0	0	2	1
Poor home conditions	2	3	2	2	5	14	3
Risk of neglect	5	2	5	1	19	32	8
Potential battered baby	2	7	2	0	14	25	6
Total number of times	99	69	85	63	93	409	100

NOTE: The principal reason was either the sole reason where only one reason was given, or the first reason where more than one was given. Hence the total number of times each reason was given in each Social Work Area corresponds to the number of children in each Area, and likewise the total for the Borough to the number of children in the study.

ATTACHMENT I(c): Analysis of All Reasons for Admission

Reason	Number of times each reason was given in:					Total	% in LBW
	Area B	Area D	Area A	Area C	Area E		
Unsupported parent	71	42	67	44	54	278	53
Medical (parent)	15	18	13	14	18	78	15
Medical (child)	15	14	16	9	21	75	14
Removal from "in care"	1	1	1	0	1	4	1
Poor home conditions	2	6	11	4	11	34	6
Risk of neglect	6	2	5	3	19	35	6
Potential battered baby	3	7	2	0	14	26	5
Total number of times	113	90	115	74	138	530	100

ATTACHMENT I(d) TABLE I: Proportion of Times Each Type of Reason Was Given as Sole, Principal, and Any Reason Over the Whole Borough

Type of reason	Percentage occurrence as:		
	Sole Reason	Principal Reason	Any Reason
Unsupported parent	67	58	53
Medical problems	23	24	29
Low standard of care	9	17	17
Removal from "in care"	1	1	1
Total	100	100	100

NOTE: (a) Medical problems include those relating to either a parent or the child; (b) Low standard of child care includes poor home conditions, risk of neglect, and potential battered baby.

ATTACHMENT I (Chart I) — Breakdown of Reasons for the Whole Borough

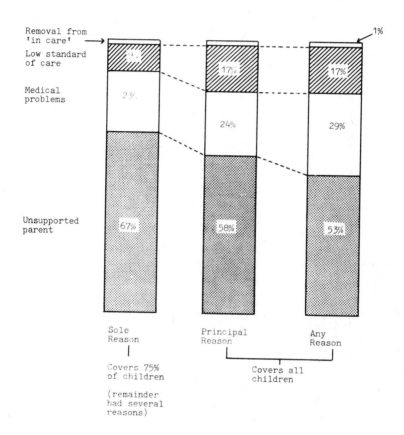

ATTACHMENT II: Number of Times Each Reason Was Given, in the Ranking Shown, in Each Day Nursery

Reason	Ranking	Area B			Area D			Area A							Area C		Area E		Total
		Nursery 1	Nursery 2	Nursery 3	Nursery 4	Nursery 5	Nursery 6	Nursery 7	Nursery 8	Nursery 9	Nursery 10	Nursery 11	Nursery 12	Nursery 13	Nursery 14	Nursery 15	Nursery 16	Nursery 17	
Unsupported Parent	Sole	36	22	8		19	35	1	1		5	6	2	13		25	16	14	203
	1st	5	2	1	2	2	3	1			4	3	1	2		1	4	4	31
	2nd	1	5	5		3	1	1				2	1	3			8	7	40
	3rd			2								1					1		4
Medical (parent)	Sole	7	4	3	2	6	1	1		1	1	1		7			2	1	30
	1st	2	2	1		2	4				1	2	1	3		1	10	4	14
	2nd			2		2								3				1	31
	3rd																		1
	4th																		2
Medical (child)	Sole	3	8	4	1	2	1				2	1		4	1		3	11	40
	1st	1	1	3		2	2				2	2		4			5	2	18
	2nd	2		1		1					5	1							17
Removal from 'in care'	Sole		1			1		1				1			1		1		2
	1st																		2
	2nd																		
Poor home conditions.	Sole	1	1	3			1					2	1	2	1		4	1	6
	1st			3							3						1	3	8
	2nd										4			1			2		14
	3rd																		6
Risk of neglect.	Sole	1	4	1							2	2		1			4	9	8
	1st	1												2			6		24
	2nd																		3
Potential battered baby.	Sole	2		1	3	2					2						3	2	13
	1st	1		1													9		12
	2nd																		1
	3rd																		

212

SUMMARY OF RESEARCH ACTIVITIES IN A TYPICAL FIELD AGENCY

RESEARCH

A Profile of Current Activities

(1) *Task Centred Casework:* The data collection phase of the project will continue until Christmas. After that no new project case will be taken and current cases will run their course. There will be a continuing commitment to analysis of the information, tying up the ends and writing up the project.

A substantial part of this project, as it has developed, will be a description of the type of cases referred to an Area Office, the services supplied, and the outcome as viewed by client and social worker. For this a comparison group of clients will be needed, to demonstrate how typical, or otherwise, our project sample is. This will involve taking a random selection of clients referred to the area over the study period, and analysing these by age, sex, referred by, duration of contact and, if possible, social class and problem type. This will be undertaken by "desk research".

(2) *The Computer and an Agency Information Base:* The next six months should see continuing work on perfecting the system and improving the quality of the information held. This will include specifying further outputs and improving the effectiveness of error checks on the one hand, and comparing the computer record against source information on the other.

(3) *Area Intake Team:* This evaluation was planned in three phases:
  (a) the social workers' opinion of the organization of the Area into intake/long-term teams,
  (b) the number of cases dealt with, how long they stay open, how often a transfer of social workers is involved, and so on.
  (c) a description of the services actually given to the clients: What the client wanted; what he got; what the social worker thought was and was not achieved; and what the client thought of it. This might involve interviewing the clients at about three months after referral, to pick up actual changes resulting from intervention, some idea of permanence of the change, and a picture and opinion of hand-over arrangements at three months where this happens.

Phase a is now complete (currently being typed) and includes a review of the literature.

Phase b is now ready to be started. Some preliminary work has been undertaken but only with a view to estimating the work that would be necessary. No interviewing is involved in this stage, which could be compressed into about one month of fairly intensive work.

Phase c had originally been envisaged as starting in September/October. A good deal of specification of objectives and methods remains to be done, and the work might be expected to last over at least a seven-month period.

(4) *Need/Demand for Old Persons Homes:* This repeat study is being carried out at the request of the Social Services Committee.

It has been asked for each six months, and will therefore be a recurring commitment. There will probably be further exercises in relation to analysis of admissions to Old Persons Homes and a longitudinal study of the cohort in the repeat need/demand exercise mentioned above.

(5) *Area B — Reception Study:* This study has just got under way. It involves interviewing some 20 office callers to get their reactions to the reception arrangements in the Area Office. It was scheduled to run through August and be written up in September, but a decline in the number of callers caused the

schedule to be put back by a month to six weeks so that a very unusually slack time could be avoided in the study period.

(6) *Area C — Study of Younger Physically Handicapped:* Mr W____ is supervising three trainees on a project conceived in the area for the period immediately before they leave on secondment for professional training. This was completed in October.

(7) *Area D — Calling Points:* Research section has been asked to advise on evaluation to be carried out by the Area Office. This will involve a small periodic commitment.

(8) *Area A — Out of Hours Work:* Research section is providing help as required for an assessment of out-of-hours work undertaken by Area social workers. This involves a small periodic commitment.

(9) *Area A Adult Training Unit — Behaviour Modification:* There is a small periodic commitment in helping develop scales of assessment for use in the behaviour modification trials.

(10) *Area B — Census of Mentally Handicapped Persons:* There is a small periodic commitment, up to the end of December, in advising and assisting a G.P. trainee with an exercise in trying to identify all the mentally handicapped in the Area.

(11) *Semi-Secure Accommodation:* There is a small continuing commitment with this project organised by the Department of Psychiatry at the Hospital. The project aims to define both the need for semi-secure accommodation and the numbers involved. The field work phase of this project is drawing to an end.

(12) *Staff Turnover:* A small desk study on numbers of staff joining and leaving the department is nearing completion. The one-year period being studied ended on 30th September, 1975.

(13) *Miscellaneous Continuing Jobs:* There are normally research reports, especially on referrals, advice, etc., on statistics and returns; at the moment involvement with the redesign of the WS2; and representation on the Records Working Party.

Future Work

This is an appropriate time, therefore, to consider the research programme:

(a) Shold the intake study continue as planned?

(b) Should more emphasis be put on research which is strictly related to planning and a "no growth" budget e.g., identifying areas where work is not carried out, identifying and demonstrating need for services, evaluating novel uses of resources, examining costly areas of departmental practice?

Examples of work that might be undertaken with this in mind are:

(a) To examine characteristics of old/physically handicapped persons placed in voluntary homes.

(b) Children placed out-of-County: What is the cost of this — fees, but also travel, search time, and so on?

(c) Likewise for children in care but at home — is this planned and good for the child — or the result of not having an appropriate placement?

(d) Identify children in care making frequent moves. What are the causes and what are costs in time and money?

(e) Retrospectively trace the history of a sample of children from referral to care. Could alternative resources have prevented it?

(f) What evidence is there that staff sickness is related to stress?

(g) What is the comparative distribution of work between hospital and Area Office social workers?

(h) A reappraisal of the costs and benefits represented in relative emphasis on capital or revenue expenditure. Changes in the relative costs of buildings and staff over the past, say, five years.

Over the next few weeks it is hoped to compare these types of focus with the more "ad-hoc" commissioning of work that the Research Section has followed until now.

B3

DESCRIPTION OF THE FUNCTION OF RESEARCH IN A SERVICE AGENCY

THE FUNCTION OF RESEARCH

(1) In order to make good decisions about the services it provides, the Department needs information of many kinds. Some of this is best collected routinely, so that it is constantly available. Some, which is required for a specific purpose, may have to be collected by a special effort.

(2) In an ideal world the decision makers would state the impending issues well in advance, so that the best information could be made available by those who provide it. Unfortunately the hardest issues are often ones where the questions cannot even be framed until long after the collection of information should have been begun.

(3) It is the task of the research team to narrow this gap — to demand of the decision makers greater clarification of the questions at issue, and to discover sources of information to answer' these questions.

(4) When information has been defined so that routine collection is possible, the task can become an administrative one. The research team should not become encumbered by largely routine operations, although their interest in sources of information will give them a vital relationship with anyone performing these operations, and they will be concerned to help create effective information systems.

(5) Broadly the Department needs the following types of information:

  (a) *Information about the people and territory it serves*

    e.g., census data: population figures, age structure, types of employment and households

    — local studies of economic trends

    — data on specific client groups and problems relevant to the Department's work

  (b) *Information about the policy and practice of other departments and services*

    e.g., growth points; village plans

    — new roads

    — location of schools

    — location of health centres

    — numbers of housing lists; in receipt of Supplementary Benefit

    — voluntary services e.g., meals-on-wheels, "good neighbours," and other networks

  (c) *Information about the Department's own processes*

    e.g., requests for services; response (intake data)

    — who gets help; for what; for how long; who gets closed; area differences (casework studies)

    — speed of admission to residential care; quality of care; disability levels in residential care

    — cost of different systems of care

(6) Some of this is available; some is only of value when collated with other information; some needs considerable imagination to make it accessible.

Through the County Planning Department in particular, the County Council can make available much of the demographic type of information, but it is necessary to have much more effective liaison than we currently have, to know what exists, let alone extract it.

Information about policy within other departments is in theory available through Chief Officers and County Minutes; but again effective liaison must occur at other levels through routine exchange of ideas while they are at a formative or even speculative stage.

Much information about the Department's own processes goes uncollected for want of simple monitoring devices. We should be able to say at the drop of a hat how many 90-year-olds we have in homes for the elderly, or how many foster parents are currently not used. At present every attempt at retrieval of these facts is a major imposition on staff.

The same applies to information about outside services. We receive some data which lies fallow, and could obtain more if we were clear what we wanted.

Information of certain kinds can only be obtained by special surveys or studies. Qualitative information in particular (how well do we talk to the blind?); or information about dynamic processes (do social workers in area X play a real part in decision-making?) can only be obtained by special projects.

(7) In the absence of any other form of information service, it will clearly be one task of the research team:

   (a) to discover what information is available through other departments, organisations, libraries, and publications

   (b) to maintain channels of communication with other information officers locally and nationally

   (c) to present important information to the Department in a manageable form, for both managerial and professional functions

   (d) to advise about ways of monitoring the organisation

   (e) to help design projects, some of which will be undertaken by others

(8) The principal task of the research team, however, will be to take up those issues which are of greatest concern at a given time to the decision makers. The qualities required in the research section will depend on this agenda — but it also has a role in defining it.

(9) The skills required for such a range of activities are quite varied. At times the skills of a statistician or survey designer are needed; at others skill in interpreting collections of facts and in presenting them to others; skill in helping others to ask the right questions, or to clarify options; skill in evaluating services and skill in interpreting financial aspects. Each project requires a different combination of skills and at any one time several projects are in hand. Some are long-term projects requiring occasional

short bursts of activity; some are recurring monitoring exercises requiring regular analysis; some are special schemes needing full-time attention for several weeks and others are quite limited operations producing information for a particular purpose. Because of this variety, the research section has to turn its attention week by week to quite diverse operations and make use of help from other sources.

(10) It is desirable from many points of view that operational staff should be involved in research projects. Much "soft" data and qualitative information can only be obtained in discussion with social work staff; it is helpful, too, for operational staff to gain experience of research processes; and above all this will help divisions to feel part of the planning process. Similarly, it is desirable to draw on the skills built into the administrative sections of the department and on those in other departments.

(11) It is important for the research section to maintain a detached position when interpreting data, but in a practical setting such as social services, their role is also to facilitate change by helping others to make choices on the basis of partial evidence in a political arena. There is a need, therefore, to explore and resolve policy issues in cooperation with others and to provide an advisory service to colleagues willing to participate in research.

JOB DESCRIPTION OF A
SENIOR RESEARCH OFFICER
IN ONE OF THE FIELD AGENCIES

SENIOR RESEARCH OFFICER JOB SPECIFICATIONS

(1) *General duties*

The provision of:

  (a) sound basic material on which systematic planning for social services can confidently proceed (thus achieving better informed management decision making)

  (b) assistance in programming the work of the department

Note: Information within the remit of the research officer's work covers statistical data (both non financial and financial), research data (quantitative and qualitative), and other qualitative material.

(2) *Specific duties*

  (a) The collection, processing, analysis, interpretation, presentation and dissemination of information relevant to the development of social services. This could include, for example:

    (1) the provision of regular statistics on the work of the department relating to financial and non financial data

    (2) the periodic assessment of social needs of the Borough (but excluding those needs which are outside the remit of the social services department)

    (3) consideration of the relevance of published statistics and demographic data

    (4) the consideration of the relevance of research findings and other published material within research officer's remit

(5) in cooperation with Finance Officer preparation of cost effectiveness and cost-benefit studies

(6) development of measurements of output

(b) advising on (a) above where these activities are undertaken by other staff in the department, and assisting in the formation of information needs.

(c) making a positive contribution towards the following periodic department activities:

(1) determination of priorities

(2) preparation of plans and programmes

(3) evaluation of the use of resources and assessment of alternatives in terms of both what should be evaluated and how it may be evaluated

(4) assistance in evaluation and follow-up of plans

(5) assessment of departmental performance in relation to its main objectives

(6) review of the department's main objectives

(7) the formulation and assessment of departmental policy and practice

(d) the development of computer application to social services

(e) participation in any relevant surveys

(3) *Relationships*

(a) to deputy director for research

(b) to other staff in the research section

(c) with other staff in the department:

(1) collateral ⎫
(2) service giving ⎬ according to the situation

(3) exercising staff role where the collection of data is involved, including financial data

(d) with staff outside the department:

(1) collateral ⎫
(2) service giving ⎬ according to the situation
(3) service seeking ⎭

(4) The research officer decides (within agreed departmental policy)

(a) what information to collect, and how best to collect and use the information — consulting and involving colleagues where appropriate, and taking account of expressed information needs. This would include decisions on, for example:

(1) the frequency of collection (ongoing, periodic, once-off, etc.)

(2) the method of collection (routine procedures, periodic procedures, special projects using research techniques, etc.)

(3) the source of collection (primary, e.g., departmental records or secondary, e.g., published material, etc.)

(4) the storage and methods of retrieving information (in consultation with the training officer where this impinges on her responsibility for the departmental library)

(b) in consultation with colleagues, the details of research programme of the section

(c) what advice to offer colleagues, where relevant on information-gathering, where this is done outside the research section (e.g., social workers or community workers carrying out their own research project)

(d) what advice to give on the use of information and on the information needs of the department

(e) what advice to give in order to contribute towards the departmental activities listed under 2(c) above

(f) what advice to give on the development of computer application to social services

(g) when to consult outside bodies on a particular problem, who to consult, whether to accept, and how to use the advice and information so gained

(h) on the degree to which he/she involves him/herself in assisting outside bodies in their information-gathering activities

(i) what statistical information to give other borough departments concerning the work of the social services department

(j) how to deploy staff in the research section

(k) on the appointment of research section staff

(5) Such other related duties as the Department of Social Services may from time to time decide.

INDEX

ABOUT THE AUTHOR

Jack Rothman has been a researcher, teacher, and practitioner in the human services for over 25 years. A continuing theme in his work has been the systematic application of social science knowledge to contemporary issues of policy and practice. He holds a Ph.D. in social psychology from Columbia University and an M.S.W. from Ohio State University. His main areas of writing have included organizational innovation and change, community organization, and race and ethnic relations. Data for this book were gathered while Professor Rothman was a Fulbright-Hayes Senior Research Fellow in Great Britain. Dr. Rothman is professor at the School of Social Work, University of Michigan. He has also taught at the University of Pittsburgh and has lectured in Europe and the Near East. He is author of thirteen previous books.